Pickin' A Chicken
(A No Nonsense Guide)

Julie Felton
(A No Nonsense Gal)

In memory of Frieda...
my sweet little red hen.

CONTENTS

PREFACE

So, you have chicken fever, do you? I, too, suffered from this malady for a couple of years before I took the plunge and got a few chickens of my own. Now, there's no turning back… and I couldn't be happier. In fact, I wish I would have done it sooner.

Before I carried my first little balls of fluff home in a cardboard, carry-out type box from my local farm supply store, I did my research. I knew that chicken keeping was a big responsibility and did not take it lightly. These little creatures would depend on me to keep them safe, healthy and happy. Whether they liked it or not, I would be their new mama. Determined to not let them down, I read everything I could get my hands on. My research made me realize there were many things I never even thought to consider. Suddenly, keeping a few hens seemed like a daunting task. Well, it doesn't have to be that way. Chickens are not difficult to care for and do not take as much time as you might think. I promise!

PESKY DETAILS

Groan if you must, but there are a few things you need to consider before starting your flock. The most important of these is whether or not your neighborhood allows chickens. More and more communities are warming up to the idea of backyard flocks. However, many more are opposed to backyard chicken keeping. Contact your local officials regarding the zoning laws of your community.

If your community allows chickens, the next step is to find out how many chickens you will be able to keep and if there are rules regarding their housing. In communities that welcome chickens, the number of female chickens allowed is usually 3-6. No roosters! They're just too darn noisy. In other communities, one of the conditions of keeping chickens is getting permission from your next door neighbors. Each community is different and has its own set of rules and conditions, which is why it is very important to work out the details before you set your heart on keeping chickens in your backyard.

Another important consideration is time. While chickens don't take a lot of time to care for, at the very least, they will need your attention at the beginning and the end of each day. If you are able to check on them several

3

times throughout the day, that's even better. Their needs are basic and take very little time to meet. They need a steady supply of water and food, egg collection at least once a day, and maybe a few minutes of light coop cleaning. If you have more time, give them supervised free range time and let them scratch for bugs, weeds, and grubs in the yard once or twice a day. They are a joy to watch and quite comical. There's nothing more relaxing and entertaining than chicken-watching at the end of the day.

Then, there's the money issue. Chickens are fairly inexpensive animals to keep. Of course, their initial set-up (housing, run fencing, feeding supplies, etc.) can be quite costly if you get caught up in the hype and don't keep an eye on your spending. For most backyard chicken enthusiasts, housing is the biggest expense. It's easy to start out with a simple coop plan and end up with an extravagant, and expensive, chicken condo. Believe me! If you are lucky enough to already have safe, secure housing on your property to protect your chickens from predators and the elements, you will save a considerable amount of money. However, if you need to build or purchase a coop, they can range from free (using recycled materials) to hundreds, or even thousands, of dollars. Makes you think twice about all of those "inexpensive" eggs that will soon be rolling in, doesn't it? Feed is another expense. I spend about $30 a month on feed for my six chickens. I supplement that with treats such as mealworms, cracked corn, vegetable scraps, non-citrus fruit, old corn cobs, etc. Some of these treats are free, as they are scraps. Others are purchased from my local feed store. Though, I do admit to buying a head of cabbage occasionally for the girls. It keeps them entertained.

DETERMINE YOUR NEEDS

Before you run to the feed store and scoop up a handful of cute little chicks, you need to decide why you want chickens in the first place. If you skip this important step, you could end up with the wrong breed, which would be bad for both you and your new feathered friends. So, start off on the right foot and give some thought to the role your new chicks will play in your life.

All chickens are not created equal. Some chickens are strictly show birds. Others are excellent layers. A few are dual purpose breeds, meaning they are good for both meat and eggs. There are hundreds of chicken breeds and so many things to consider. Why do *you* want chickens? These are a few of the most popular reasons people raise chickens:

- Eggs
- Meat
- Meat and Eggs
- For Exhibition
- As Pets

Once you decide what purpose your feathered friends will serve, there are other things you need to consider that will help narrow down your choices such as:

- How many eggs do you want per day?
- Do you have an egg color preference?
- Do you want friendly chickens that make good pets?
- Do you want fancy chickens?
- Do you live in an area with extremely cold winters or hot summers?
- Would you like to raise heritage chickens, hybrids or run of the mill production chickens?

Oh my. So many questions. Not to worry! I will guide you step by step through the chicken selection process and will arm you with useful information about everything you should consider when choosing a chicken breed, including climate considerations, plumage styles, laying rates, temperaments, and so much more. I will also give you examples of breeds that work in a variety of situations. By the end of this book you will be able to pick the perfect chicken with confidence.

CHICKEN TERMINOLOGY

Before we get started on the chicken selection process, there are a few chicken related terms you should know, as many of them will be mentioned throughout the book.

Bantam: Also called a banty. It is a small variety of chicken approximately 1/4 to 1/2 the size of a standard size chicken.

Beard: Bunched feathers under a chicken's chin that resemble a beard. Found in Ameraucana, Faverolles, and Houda, among others.

Booted: A chicken with extravagant feathers on its feet and hock joints.

Breeders: Chickens that lay fertile eggs.

Broiler: A chicken bred for its meat. They are processed at 9-12 weeks old and weigh 2.5-3.5 pounds. Also called a fryer.

Broody: A hen is said to "go broody" when she insists on sitting on her eggs to hatch them. Unless you want to raise chickens from eggs, a broody hen can be a problem. While she is broody, she will not lay eggs and will spend most of her time in the nesting box, leaving only to eat and drink. She will also pluck the feathers from her chest and use them to line her nesting box. Broodiness has been bred out of many modern breeds, though there are still some breeds known for their broodiness.

Cape: The set of long feathers (hackles) on a chicken's neck.

Capon: A castrated rooster.

Chick: A male or female baby chicken.

Classification (Class): Purebred chickens grouped according to their place of origin. American, Asiatic, Continental, English, Mediterranean, and All Other Standard Breeds are classifications for standard breeds. Bantam classifications include Single Comb Clean Legged, Rose Comb Clean Legged, All Other Comb Clean Legged, Feather Legged, and Game Bantam.

Clean Legged: Having no feathers on the shanks.

Cockerel: A male chicken less than one year old.

Comb. The fleshy pink or red crown on a chicken's head. Comb styles vary among breeds and range from large and floppy to close-cropped and small.

Crest: A puff of feathers on top of a chicken's head. Also called a top knot.

Crossbreed: The offspring of a hen and rooster of two different breeds.

Dual Purpose: A chicken used for both meat and eggs.

Ear Lobe: The fleshy part just below the ear hole. Typically, chickens with white ear lobes lay white eggs and chickens with colored ear lobes lay brown eggs.

Exhibition Breed: A breed of chicken kept mainly for its beauty.

Feather Legged: Having feathers on the legs.

Feed-to-egg conversion: How much a chicken eats in relation to the number of eggs she produces. Chickens with a good feed-to-egg conversion will save you money on feed because they eat less and produce more.

Feed-to-meat conversion: How much a chicken eats in relation to the amount of meat he/she produces. Chickens with a good feed-to-meat conversion will save you money on feed because they eat less and produce more.

Frizell: Feathers that curl at the ends rather than being flat. Also a curly feathered breed of chicken.

Hackles: Cape feathers on a rooster.

Hatching Eggs: Eggs from females who have been kept with a rooster.

Hen: A female chicken that is one year old.

Heritage: A chicken whose genetic line can be traced back multiple generations and whose traits meet the APA Standard of Perfection guidelines for the breed.

Hybrid: The offspring of a hen and rooster of different breed who might also be from crossbred birds.

Layers: Adult female chickens who are laying eggs. Also known as laying hens.

Muff: Feathers that stick out from both sides of the face under the chin. Also called whiskers.

Plumage: The feathers covering a chicken.

Point of Lay (POL): - Point of lay chickens are females 16-18 weeks old who are getting ready to start laying eggs. Hybrids will lay within two or three weeks. Traditional breeds may take longer because they tend to be heavier and take longer to mature.

Pullet: A female chicken that is less than one year old.

Purebred: The offspring of a hen and rooster of the same breed.

Roaster: A 4-6 pound cockerel or pullet used for roasting whole in the oven.

Rooster: A male chicken. Also called a cock.

Saddle: The part of a chicken's back right before the tail.

Sexed: Newly hatched chicks that have been sorted into pullets (girls) and cockerels (boys).

Sex-link: A chicken produced by a hen and rooster of two different breeds. The offspring of these two breeds can be sexed based on their color or patterns immediately after hatching. Females are one color/pattern and males another.

Shank: The area between the claw and the first joint on a chicken's leg.

Sickles: Long, curved tail feathers on certain breeds of roosters.

Standard: A description of the ideal traits of a breed.

Straight Run: Chicks that have not been sexed. When you purchase straight run chicks, you will most likely get both male and female chicks. Also called unsexed or "as hatched."

Variety: A breed subdivision according to color, comb style, etc.

RAISING CHICKENS FOR EGGS

If you are like most people, you want chickens for their delicious and nutritious eggs. There are many breeds that will meet your needs. They include everything from bantams (small chickens that lay small eggs) to Jersey Giants (the largest chicken breed). There are chickens that lay brown eggs, white eggs, and even blue and green eggs. Some chickens will give you nearly an egg a day while others will only give you an egg a week. Do you see why it is important to make sure you choose the right breed? Imagine owning six heavy layers that churn out a dozen eggs every couple of days when you only need a few table eggs here and there. The good thing about making this purchase error is that friends, family and neighbors will be happy to take the extra eggs off of your hands. However, if you have a family of five and you purchase a flock of bantams to support your heavy egg usage, you will be very disappointed to discover that they do not lay on a daily basis and that their eggs are smaller than those of standard size chickens.

By the way, hens do not need a rooster to lay eggs. They lay eggs with or without a rooster in the flock. A rooster is only necessary if you want fertilized eggs for hatching.

Lay rates will vary from season to season and will also depend on feed, free range time, and flock health. In other words, there's no way to predict exactly how many eggs your chickens will lay. However, it is possible to give a general guideline, which is what I have done here. If it is stated that a chicken is an excellent layer, it could lay anywhere from 5-7 eggs per week. If the breed is listed as a good layer, it could lay 3-5 per week. A fair layer lays 2-3 per week and a poor layer lays 1 or less per week.

There is also no way to predict the exact color of the eggs your chickens will lay. For example, Marans, known for their deep coppery brown eggs, sometimes lay eggs that are a shade or two lighter than the standard. The color of the eggs you get will depend on the breeder you purchased your chickens from, as some characteristics have been bred back.

The following are some of the most popular, dependable, egg laying breeds.

AMERAUCANA: Sometimes confused with Easter Eggers or Americanas. Unlike these mixed breed birds, Ameraucanas are a purebred breed. Be sure to check the spelling before you accidentally purchase an Americana thinking that it is an Ameraucana.
Size: 5 lbs. (female), 6 lbs. (male)
Number of eggs per week: Good
Egg Color: Green or Blue
Egg Size: Large
Classification: All Other
Comb Style: Pea
Temperament: Calm and not afraid of people.
Broody: Yes

Colors: Black, Blue, Blue-wheaten, Brown-red, Buff, Silver, Wheaten, White

ANCONA: The Ancona gets its name from its original breeding place, Ancona, Italy. They arrived in the United States in the late 1800's and became a popular breed.

Size: 4 lbs. (female), 6 lbs. (male)

Number of eggs per week: Excellent

Egg Color: White

Egg Size: Large

Classification: Mediterranean

Comb Style: Rose and Single

Temperament: Have some wild tendencies and are a bit flighty.

Broody: No

Color: Black with white mottling.

ANDALUSIAN: This breed originated in the Andalucia region of Spain. Oddly, when two blues are bred, the result is some whites and some blacks, making this breed rare except among poultry enthusiasts.

Size: 5 lbs. (female), 7 lbs. (male)

Number of eggs per week: Good

Egg Color: White

Egg Size: Large

Classification: Mediterranean

Comb Style: Single

Temperament: Flighty

Broody: No

Colors: The color recognized by the American Poultry Association is blue. They also can be black or mottled.

APPENZELLER: The Appenzeller originated in the Appenzell region of Switzerland. There are two types of Appenzellers – Spitzhauben and Barthuhner. The Spitzhauben is more popular in North America. These chickens sport a comical, yet interesting crest of feathers on their heads.

Size: 3 lbs. (female), 4 lbs. (male)

Number of eggs per week: Good

Egg Color: White

Egg Size: Medium

Classification: Not recognized

Comb Style: V-shaped

Temperament: Can be very friendly once trained.

Broody: No

Color: White with black spots.

AUSTRALORP: This breed originated in Australia, as the name suggests, and was developed from England's Black Orpington. In the 1920's, it set a world record for most eggs laid in a year (364).

Size: 6 lbs. (female), 8 lbs. (male)

Number of eggs per week: Excellent

Egg Color: Brown

Egg Size: Large

Classification: English

Comb Style: Single

Temperament: Sweet, good natured chickens that make excellent pets and are good around children.

Broody: Sometimes.

Color: Shiny black feathers with iridescent green and purple highlights that glisten in sunlight.

BARNEVELDER: Known for its dark, chocolate colored eggs, the Barnevelder originated in the Dutch town of Barneveld. Over the years, breeders have not concentrated on egg color and their dark brown eggs are not as dark as they once were.

Size: 6 lbs. (female), 7 lbs. (male)

Number of eggs per week: Good

Egg Color: Dark Brown

Egg Size: Large

Classification: Continental

Comb Style: Single

Temperament: Lively and friendly.

Broody: Sometimes

Colors: Double-laced Partridge, Blue-laced, White, Black

BLACK STAR: This breed is a sex-link, meaning that it can be sexed based on its color immediately after hatching. Typically, they are a cross between a Barred Plymouth Rock female and a Rhode Island Red male, though other crosses exist. Male chicks are black with a white spot on their heads while female chicks are solid black. This breed sometimes goes by the names Black Rock or Black Sex Link. Sex link chickens are not recommended as breeding stock since there is no way to know which characteristics they will pass along to their offspring.

Size: 5 lbs. (female), 7 lbs. (male)

Number of eggs per week: Excellent

Classification: Not recognized

Egg Color: Brown

Egg Size: Large

Comb Style: Single

Temperament: Docile and friendly. Make good pets.

Broody: No

Color: Black with copper tints.

BRAHMA: One of the larger breeds, this chicken is known as The Gentle Giant because of its exceptionally calm, friendly demeanor.

Size: 9 lbs. (female), 12 lbs. (male)

Number of eggs per week: Good

Egg Color: Brown

Egg Size: Large

Classification: Asiatic

Comb Style: Pea

Temperament: Extremely gentle and tame.

Broody: Yes

Colors: Light, Dark, Buff

BUCKEYE: The Buckeye is the only American breed to be developed by a woman. Nettie Metcalf of Warren, Ohio, developed these winter-hardy layers in late 19th century. The Buckeye is a pea combed variety of the Rhode Island Red, and happens to be the only pea combed breed of American origin. As odd as it sounds, they are known for being good mousers.

Size: 5 lbs. (female), 9 lbs. (male)

Number of eggs per week: Good

Egg Color: Brown

Egg Size: Large

Classification: American

Comb Style: Pea

Temperament: Calm, friendly and easy to handle.

Broody: Sometimes

Color: Deep Brown

CALIFORNIA GRAY: Cross between a White Leghorn and a Barred Plymouth Rock that was developed in California in the 1930's.

Size: 4 lbs. (female), 5 lbs. (male)

Number of eggs per week: Good

Egg Color: White

Egg Size: Large

Classification: Not recognized

Comb Style: Single

Temperament: Docile and can be held.

Broody: No

Color: Barred Gray/White

CALIFORNIA WHITE: Cross between a White Leghorn hen and a California Gray rooster.

Size: 5 lbs. (female), 7 lbs. (male)

Number of eggs per week: Excellent

Egg Color: White

Egg Size: Large

Classification: Not recognized

Comb Style: Single

Temperament: Quiet and easy to handle.

Broody: No

Color: White

CATALANA: The Catalana was developed in the district of Catalonia Spain, which is near Barcelona. More popular in South American and Spain than in the United States.

Size: 6 lbs. (female), 8 lbs. (male)

Number of eggs per week: Good

Egg Color: White to tinted

Egg Size: Medium

Classification: Mediterranean

Comb Style: Single

Temperament: Active and avoids people.

Broody: No

Color: Buff

CHANTECLER: Known as Canada's breed, the Chantecler was developed by Brother Wilfred Chatalain of the Oka Agricultural Institute in Quebec. It is a bit chubby and a great choice for those in a cold climate.

Size: 6 lbs. (female), 8 lbs. (male)

Number of eggs per week: Good

Egg Color: Brown

Egg Size: Large

Classification: American

Comb Style: Cushion

Temperament: Quiet and easy to handle.

Broody: Yes

Colors: White, Buff, Partridge

DOMINQUE: This heritage breed is sometimes confused with a Barred Rock because they both have a barred pattern. The difference between the two breeds is that the Dominique has a rose comb while the Barred Rock has a single comb. Also goes by the name Dominiker.

Size: 5 lbs. (female), 7 lbs. (male)

Number of eggs per week: Good

Egg Color: Brown

Egg Size: Medium

Classification: American

Comb Style: Rose

Temperament: Calm

Broody: Yes

Colors: Barred black and white.

DELAWARE: This breed originates from Delaware. It was once quite common, but is now endangered.

Size: 6 lbs. (female), 8 lbs. (male)

Number of eggs per week: Good

Egg Color: Brown

Egg Size: Large

Classification: American

Comb Style: Single

Temperament: Friendly and calm.

Broody: Yes

Color: White body with light black barring on the hackle, wings and tail.

DORKING: It is believed that the Dorking originated in Italy and dates back to the days of the Roman Empire. This makes it one of the oldest

English breeds. What makes this bird unique is the fact that it has five toes rather than the standard four.

Size: 7 lbs. (female), 9 lbs. (male)

Number of eggs per week: Good

Egg Color: White

Egg Size: Large

Classification: English

Comb Style: Rose and Single

Temperament: Quiet and calm.

Broody: Yes

Colors: White, Dark, Silver Grey, Cuckoo, Red (extremely rare)

FAVEROLLE: This breed is strangely beautiful with its muffs, beard and feathered legs. It also has five toes as opposed to the typical four.

Size: 6 lbs. (female), 8 lbs. (male)

Number of eggs per week: Good

Egg Color: Creamy to light brown

Egg Size: Medium

Classification: Continental

Comb Style: Single

Temperament: Shy and sweet.

Broody: Yes

Colors: Salmon, White

HOLLAND: This breed was NOT developed in Holland. In fact, it was created in New Jersey. One of the breeds used in its development, however, was imported from Holland.

Size: 6 lbs. (female), 8 lbs. (male)

Number of eggs per week: Good

Egg Color: White

Egg Size: Large

Classification: American

Comb Style: Single

Temperament: Calm and even tempered.

Broody: Sometimes

Colors: White, Barred

JERSEY GIANT: The Jersey Giant is the largest chicken breed available. As its name implies, it was developed in New Jersey.

Size: 10 lbs. (female), 13 lbs. (male)

Number of eggs per week: Good

Egg Color: Brown

Egg Size: Extra Large

Classification: American

Comb Style: Single

Temperament: Gentle

Broody: Sometimes

Colors: Black, White

LA FLECHE: This French breed is also known as the "Devil Bird" because its V-shaped comb resembles horns.

Size: 6 lbs. (female), 8 lbs. (male)

Number of eggs per week: Good

Egg Color: White

Egg Size: Large

Classification: Continental

Comb Style: V-Shaped

Temperament: Does not like human contact and acts slightly wild.

Broody: No

Colors: Its official color is black, though it also comes in blue, white, and cuckoo.

LEGHORN: Because they are prolific layers, most commercially produced eggs come from Leghorns. They originated in Italy and get their name from Livorno (also known as Leghorn).

Size: 4 lbs. (female), 5 lbs. (male)

Number of eggs per week: Excellent

Egg Color: White

Egg Size: Large

Classification: Mediterranean

Comb Style: White birds have single combs. Some other colors have rose combs.

Temperament: Slightly nervous and can be flighty. Not the best choice if you are looking for a bird you can interact with easily. Leghorns are used as a cross in many modern breeds and when bred with a calmer bird, the temperament of their offspring improves.

Broody: No

Colors: Most commonly brown or white. Buff, black, silver, and other colors are available, though rare.

MARAN: Developed in France, this breed is prized for its beautiful dark brown, coppery eggs.

Size: 7 lbs. (female), 8 lbs. (male)

Number of eggs per week: Good

Egg Color: Dark Brown

Egg Size: Large

Classification: Continental

Comb Style: Single

Temperament: Calm and quiet.

Broody: Yes

Colors: Black, Cuckoo

MINORCA: This breed gets its name from the Island of Minorca off the coast of Spain. It is sometimes called the "Red Faced Black Chicken" because of its red face and large red wattle and comb.

Size: 7 lbs. (female), 9 lbs. (male)

Number of eggs per week: Excellent

Egg Color: White

Egg Size: Extra Large

Classification: Mediterranean

Comb Style: Single and Rose

Temperament: Avoids human contact.

Broody: No

Colors: Black, White, Buff

NAKED NECK: As its name implies, this odd looking chicken doesn't have feathers on its neck. In fact, it has almost half the feathers of other breeds its size. Also known as a Turken.

Size: 6 lbs. (female), 8 lbs. (male)

Number of eggs per week: Good

Egg Color: Tinted to Light Brown

Egg Size: Medium

Classification: All Other

Comb Style: Single

Temperament: Calm, active, yet easy to handle.

Broody: Yes

Colors: Black, white and red are recognized by the American Poultry Association. Other varieties are blue, cuckoo, or barred.

ORPINGTON: One of the smartest breeds. Believe it or not, some owners claim they are able to teach their Orpington tricks.

Size: 8 lbs. (female), 10 lbs. (male)

Number of eggs per week: Good

Egg Color: Light Brown

Egg Size: Large

Classification: English

Comb Style: Single

Temperament: Exceptionally docile.

Broody: Sometimes

Colors: The original colors of black, white, buff, and blue are the most popular. Other colors are available and are still being developed.

PENEDESENCA: Unlike most chickens with white earlobes, this Spanish breed does not lay white eggs. In fact, they are known for their beautiful dark brown eggs.

Size: 4 lbs. (female), 5 lbs. (male)

Number of eggs per week: Good

Egg Color: Dark Brown

Egg Size: Medium

Classification: Not recognized

Comb Style: Carnation

Temperament: Flighty and excitable.

Broody: Yes

Colors: Creole, Wheaten, Partridge, Black

PLYMOUTH ROCK: Known as "the chicken your grandma had", Plymouth Rocks originated in the United States and get their name from the town of Plymouth. After WWII, they became the most popular breed in America.

Size: 7 lbs. (female), 9 lbs. (male)

Number of eggs per week: Good

Classification: American

Egg Color: Brown

Egg Size: Large

Comb Style: Single

Temperament: Docile and friendly.

Broody: Yes. Make good mothers.

Colors: They come in several varieties, barred (black with white "barring"), buff and white being the most common. Other colors are partridge, silver laced, blue, and Columbian.

POLISH: This breed is known for its comical bouffant crest feathers that give it a Phyllis Diller look. Comes in bearded and beardless varieties.

Size: 4 lbs. (female), 6 lbs. (male)

Number of eggs per week: Good

Egg Color: White

Egg Size: Medium

Classification: Continental

Comb Style: V-Shaped

Temperament: Somewhat flighty and often on the bottom of the pecking order.

Broody: No

Colors: Black, White, Golden, Silver, Buff Laced

REDCAP: This bird sports a huge red comb, hence its name. Also known as the Derbyshire Redcap.

Size: 6 lbs. (female), 7 lbs. (male)

Number of eggs per week: Good

Egg Color: White

Egg Size: Medium

Classification: English

Comb Style: Rose

Temperament: Somewhat wild.

Broody: No

Color: Reddish brown to Bluish-Black

RED STAR: This breed is a sex-link, meaning that it can be sexed based on its color immediately after hatching. Female chicks are buff or brown/red and male chicks are white. Red Stars are created by crossing a red hen with a White Rock, Silver Laced Wyandotte, Delaware, or Rhode Island White. Unlike many breeds, they will produce heavily through hot and cold weather. They sometimes go by the names Production Red, Golden Buff, Comet, Golden Comet, Golden Sex Link, and Isa Brown. Sex link chickens are not recommended as breeding stock since there is no way to know which characteristics they will pass along to their offspring.

Size: 5 lbs. (female), 6 lbs. (male)

Number of eggs per week: Excellent

Egg Color: Brown

Egg Size: Large to Extra Large

Classification: Not recognized

Comb Style: Single

Temperament: Easy going.

Broody: No

Color: Reddish brown with small areas of white sprinkled throughout.

RHODE ISLAND RED or WHITE: The official state bird of Rhode Island. It dates back to the mid 1840's, making it one of the oldest breeds in America.

Size: 6 lbs. (female), 8 lbs. (male)

Number of eggs per week: Excellent

Egg Color: Brown

Egg Size: Large

Classification: American

Comb Style: Single

Temperament: Good natured and docile.

Broody: No

Colors: Reddish-brown. There is also a White Rhode Island, though not as common.

SICILIAN BUTTERCUP: This bird comes from Sicily and wears a cup shaped comb.

Size: 5 lbs. (female), 6 lbs. (male)

Number of eggs per week: Good

Egg Color: White

Egg Size: Medium

Classification: Mediterranean

Comb Style: Buttercup

Temperament: Flighty

Broody: No

Color: Buff with black spots.

SPANISH: An aristocrat in the chicken world, this breed is known for its stunning white face and earlobes against greenish, black plumage. Also known as White-Faced Black Spanish, Spanish White Ear, or Clown Face

Size: 6 lbs. (female), 8 lbs. (male)

Number of eggs per week: Good

Egg Color: White

Egg Size: Large

Classification: Mediterranean

Comb Style: Single

Temperament: Flighty

Broody: No

Color: Black with white face.

WELSUMMER (or WELSUMER): This breed takes its name from the village of Welsum, Holland. They lay dark brown eggs, often with speckles. Incidentally, the rooster on the Corn Flakes box was a Welsummer.

Size: 6 lbs. (female), 7 lbs. (male)

Number of eggs per week: Good

Egg Color: Brown

Egg Size: Large

Classification: Continental

Comb Style: Single

Temperament: Docile, intelligent and easy to handle.

Broody: Sometimes

Color: Red Partridge

WYANDOTTE: An American breed that is a favorite among backyard chickens keepers because of the large number of color possibilities.

Size: 6 lbs. (female), 8 lbs. (male)

Number of eggs per week: Good

Egg Color: Brown or tinted

Egg Size: Large

Classification: American

Comb Style: Rose

Temperament: Friendly and make good pets.

Broody: Sometimes

Colors: They come in seventeen colors. The most common being silver laced, golden laced, white, black, buff, partridge, silver penciled, Columbian, and blue.

RAISING CHICKENS FOR MEAT

It is possible to use all hens and roosters for meat. Many times, people butcher their hens and roosters that, for a variety of reasons, have been culled from the flock. However, these birds will have smaller breasts and less meat overall. Some roosters are caponized (castrated) when they are young and are raised for their meat, which is more tender and flavorful than a rooster that has not been caponized.

There is a significant difference between laying birds and meat birds (also known as broilers). Most modern meat breeds are hybrids developed to have more breast meat and to grow quickly, while laying breeds spend their energy on producing eggs and less on building body mass. Meat breeds do lay eggs if raised to maturity, but not as frequently as laying chickens. Also, the eggs they lay are generally smaller.

By far, the most popular cross for meat production is the White Cornish/White Plymouth Rock cross. In as little as 6 weeks they will reach 4-5 lbs. Given 8-12 weeks, they will reach 6-10 lbs. Because of their fast growth rate and excellent feed conversion, this is the bird typically found at a grocery store. Their fast growth rate does not come without problems, however. They sometimes get too heavy, too fast, and have problems standing or suffer from heart failure.

Many times, meat birds are fed high protein feed only. This is the fastest method to produce a meaty bird, though it doesn't produce the most flavorful meat. For those who choose to let their meat birds free range on bugs and grasses, growth will be slower but the end result will be more delicious meat.

Important side note: If you plan on raising meat birds, I highly suggest not naming them!

The following are some of the most popular meat breeds.

CORNISH: These stocky birds originated in Cornwall, England. If you buy chicken from a supermarket, most likely it came from Cornish birds that were crossed with a White Plymouth Rock. Also known as Indian Game.

Size: 8 lbs. (female), 10 lbs. (male)

Number of eggs per week: Poor

Egg Color: Light Brown

Egg Size: Small

Classification: English

Comb Style: Pea

Temperament: Slow, docile and noisy.

Broody: No

Colors: White, Dark, White Laced, Red, Buff

CORNISH CROSS (Cornish X Rock): These birds are cross between a white Cornish and a white Plymouth Rock. Due to their rapid growth and efficient use of feed, the Cornish Cross is the industry standard for meat production. They do not come without problems, however. Their fast growth subjects them to foot and heart issues. Not recommended for altitudes above 5000 feet. Also called Cornish/Rocks.

Size: 3 lbs. (female), 4 lbs. (male)

Number of eggs per week: Poor

Egg Color: Brown

Egg Size: Small

Classification: Not recognized

Comb Style: Pea

Temperament: Slow and lack energy. Sometimes they even eat sitting down.

Broody: No

Color: White

The following breeds used to belong exclusively to the meat bird group but are now dual purpose, meaning they arc recommended for both their meat and eggs. Dual purpose birds will be discussed in greater detail in the next chapter. I included these in the meat bird chapter because they are excellent alternatives to the two breeds mentioned above.

JAVA: Now a critically endangered breed, the Java is one of America's oldest breeds and was instrumental in developing popular breeds such as the Plymouth Rock and Rhode Island Red, to name a few.

Size: 7 lbs. (female), 9 lbs. (male)

Number of eggs per week: Fair

Egg Color: Brown
Egg Size: Medium
Classification: American
Comb Style: Single
Temperament: Calm
Broody: Yes
Colors: Black, White, Mottled

JERSEY GIANT: The Jersey Giant is the largest chicken breed available. As its name implies, it was developed in New Jersey. These birds are heavy feeders and have a poor feed-to-meat conversion.
Size: 10 lbs. (female), 13 lbs. (male)
Number of eggs per week: Good
Egg Color: Brown
Egg Size: Extra Large
Classification: American
Comb Style: Single
Temperament: Gentle
Broody: Sometimes
Colors: Black, White

ORLOFF: The Orloff originated in Persia, though it is also known as a Russian Orloff because it was heavily promoted by Count Orlov of Russia. This breed was once classified as a continental, but is no longer a recognized breed with the American Poultry Association.
Size: 6 lbs. (female), 8 lbs. (male)
Number of eggs per week: Fair
Egg Color: Brown

Egg Size: Medium

Classification: Not recognized

Comb Style: Walnut

Temperament: Calm but avoids people.

Broody: No

Colors: Black, White, Spangled, Black-tailed Red, Mahogany, Cuckoo

DUAL PURPOSE BREEDS

Dual purpose breeds offer the best of both worlds… eggs *and* meat! They produce enough eggs for the table and, later, they… well, you know what comes later. Dual purpose breeds have less meat and smaller breasts than chickens raised exclusively for meat, such the Cornish Cross, but their meat is just as tasty. If you are looking for the ultimate bird, a dual purpose breed fits the bill.

The following are some of the most popular dual purpose breeds.

AMERAUCANA: Sometimes confused with Easter Eggers or Americanas. Unlike these mixed breed birds, Ameraucanas are a purebred breed. Be sure to check the spelling before you accidentally purchase an Americana thinking that it is an Ameraucana.
Size: 5 lbs. (female), 6 lbs. (male)
Number of eggs per week: Good
Egg Color: Green or Blue
Egg Size: Large
Classification: All Other
Comb Style: Pea

Temperament: Calm and not afraid of people.

Broody: Yes

Colors: Black, Blue, Blue-wheaten, Brown-red, Buff, Silver, Wheaten, White

AUSTRALORP: This breed originated in Australia, as the name suggests, and was developed from England's Black Orpington. In the 1920's, the breed set a world record for most eggs laid in a year (364). Size: 6 lbs. (female), 8 lbs. (male)

Number of eggs per week: Excellent

Egg Color: Brown

Egg Size: Large

Classification: English

Comb Style: Single

Temperament: Sweet, good natured chickens that make excellent pets and are good around children. They do not mind being handled and enjoy being petted.

Broody: Can be broody. Good mother.

Color: Shiny black feathers with iridescent green and purple highlights that glisten in sunlight.

BARNEVELDER: Known for its dark, chocolate colored eggs, the Barnevelder originated in the Dutch town of Barneveld. Over the years, breeders have not concentrated on egg color and their dark brown eggs are not as dark as they once were.

Size: 6 lbs. (female), 7 lbs. (male)

Number of eggs per week: Good

Egg Color: Dark Brown

Egg Size: Large

Classification: Continental

Comb Style: Single

Temperament: Lively and friendly.

Broody: Sometimes

Colors: Double-Laced Partridge, Blue-laced, White, Black

BRAHMA: One of the larger breeds, this chicken is known as The Gentle Giant because of its exceptionally calm, friendly demeanor.

Size: 9 lbs. (female), 12 lbs. (male)

Number of eggs per week: Good

Egg Color: Brown

Egg Size: Large

Classification: Asiatic

Comb Style: Pea

Temperament: Extremely gentle and tame.

Broody: Yes

Colors: Light, Dark, Buff

BUCKEYE: The Buckeye is the only American breed to be developed by a woman. Nettie Metcalf of Warren, Ohio, developed these winter-hardy layers in late 19th century. The Buckeye is a pea combed variety of the Rhode Island Red, and happens to be the only pea combed breed of American origin. As odd as it sounds, they are known for being good mousers.

Size: 5 lbs. (female), 9 lbs. (male)

Number of eggs per week: Good

Egg Color: Brown

Egg Size: Large

Classification: American

Comb Style: Pea

Temperament: Calm, friendly and easy to handle.

Broody: Sometimes

Color: Deep Brown

CALIFORNIA GRAY: Cross between a White Leghorn and a Barred Plymouth Rock that was developed in California in the 1930's.

Size: 4 lbs. (female), 5 lbs. (male)

Number of eggs per week: Good

Egg Color: White

Egg Size: Large

Classification: Not recognized

Comb Style: Single

Temperament: Docile and can be held.

Broody: No

Color: Barred Gray/White

CALIFORNIA WHITE: Cross between a White Leghorn hen and a California Gray rooster.

Size: 5 lbs. (female), 7 lbs. (male)

Number of eggs per week: Excellent

Egg Color: White

Egg Size: Large

Classification: Not recognized

Comb Style: Single

Temperament: Quiet and easy to handle.

Broody: No

Color: White

CATALANA: The Catalana was developed in the district of Catalonia Spain, which is near Barcelona. This breed is more popular in South American and Spain than in the United States.

Size: 6 lbs. (female), 8 lbs. (male)

Number of eggs per week: Good

Egg Color: White to tinted

Egg Size: Medium

Classification: Mediterranean

Comb Style: Single

Temperament: Active and avoids people.

Broody: No

Color: Buff

CHANTECLER: Known as Canada's breed, the Chantecler was developed by Brother Wilfred Chatalain of the Oka Agricultural Institute in Quebec. It is a bit chubby and a great choice for those in a cold climate.

Size: 6 lbs. (female), 8 lbs. (male)

Number of eggs per week: Good

Egg Color: Brown

Egg Size: Large

Classification: American

Comb Style: Cushion

Temperament: Quiet and easy to handle.

Broody: Yes

Colors: White, Buff, Partridge

CREVECOEUR: This beautiful bird with a showy black crest, gets its name from Crève-Coeur en Ange, a small town in Normandy, France. It is thought to be one of the oldest French breeds.

Size: 6 lbs. (female), 8 lbs. (male)

Number of eggs per week: Good

Egg Color: White

Egg Size: Medium

Classification: Continental

Comb Style: V-shaped

Temperament: Quiet and easy to handle.

Broody: No

Color: Black

DOMINQUE: This heritage breed is sometimes confused with a Barred Rock because they both have a barred pattern. The difference between the two breeds is that the Dominique has a rose comb while the Barred Rock has a single comb. Also goes by the name Dominiker.

Size: 5 lbs. (female), 7 lbs. (male)

Number of eggs per week: Good

Egg Color: Brown

Egg Size: Medium

Classification: American

Comb Style: Rose

Temperament: Calm.

Broody: Yes

Color: Barred Black/White

DELAWARE: This breed originates from Delaware. It was once quite common, but is now endangered.

Size: 6 lbs. (female), 8 lbs. (male)

Number of eggs per week: Good

Egg Color: Brown

Egg Size: Large

Classification: American

Comb Style: Single

Temperament: Friendly and calm.

Broody: Yes

Color: White body with light black barring on the hackle, wings and tail.

DORKING: It is believed that the Dorking originated in Italy and dates back to the days of the Roman Empire. This makes it one of the oldest English breeds. What makes this bird unique is the fact that it has five toes rather than the standard four.

Size: 7 lbs. (female), 9 lbs. (male)

Number of eggs per week: Good

Egg Color: White

Egg Size: Large

Classification: English

Comb Style: Rose and Single

Temperament: Quiet and calm.

Broody: Yes

Colors: White, Dark, Silver Grey, Cuckoo, Red (extremely rare)

FAVEROLLE: This breed is strangely beautiful with its muffs, beard and feathered legs. It also has five toes as opposed to the typical four.

Size: 6 lbs. (female), 8 lbs. (male)

Number of eggs per week: Good

Egg Color: Creamy to light brown

Egg Size: Medium

Classification: Continental

Comb Style: Single

Temperament: Shy and sweet.

Broody: Yes

Colors: Salmon, White

HOLLAND: This breed was NOT developed in Holland. In fact, it was created in New Jersey. One of the breeds used in its development, however, was imported from Holland.

Size: 6 lbs. (female), 8 lbs. (male)

Number of eggs per week: Good

Egg Color: White

Egg Size: Large

Classification: American

Comb Style: Single

Temperament: Calm and even tempered.

Broody: Sometimes

Colors: White, Barred

JERSEY GIANT: The Jersey Giant is the largest chicken breed available. As its name implies, it was developed in New Jersey.

Size: 10 lbs. (female), 13 lbs. (male)

Number of eggs per week: Good

Egg Color: Brown

Egg Size: Extra Large

Classification: American

Comb Style: Single

Temperament: Gentle

Broody: Sometimes

Colors: Black, White

LA FLECHE: This French breed is also known as the "Devil Bird" because its V-shaped comb resembles horns.

Size: 6 lbs. (female), 8 lbs. (male)

Number of eggs per week: Good

Egg Color: White

Egg Size: Large

Classification: Continental

Comb Style: V-Shaped

Temperament: Does not like human contact and acts slightly wild.

Broody: No

Colors: Its official color is black, though it also comes in blue, white, and cuckoo

MARAN: Developed in France, this breed is prized for its beautiful dark brown, coppery eggs.

Size: 7 lbs. (female), 8 lbs. (male)

Number of eggs per week: Good

Egg Color: Dark Brown

Egg Size: Large

Classification: Continental

Comb Style: Single

Temperament: Calm and quiet.

Broody: Yes

Colors: Black, Cuckoo.

NAKED NECK: As its name implies, this odd looking chicken doesn't have feathers on its neck. In fact, it has almost half the feathers of other breeds its size. Also known as a Turken.

Size: 6 lbs. (female), 8 lbs. (male)

Number of eggs per week: Good

Egg Color: Tinted to Light Brown

Egg Size: Medium

Classification: All Other

Comb Style: Single

Temperament: Calm, active, yet easy to handle.

Broody: Yes

Colors: Black, white and red are recognized by the American Poultry Association. Other varieties are blue, cuckoo, or barred.

NEW HAMPSHIRE: This breed was developed from the Rhode Island Red. Also known as New Hampshire Red.

Size: 6 lbs. (female), 8 lbs. (male)

Number of eggs per week: Fair

Egg Color: Brown

Egg Size: Extra Large

Classification: American

Comb Style: Single

Temperament: Docile, friendly and does not mind being handled.

Broody: Yes

Color: Light Reddish Brown

ORPINGTON: One of the smartest breeds. Believe it or not, some owners claim they are able to teach their Orpington tricks.

Size: 8 lbs. (female), 10 lbs. (male)

Number of eggs per week: Good

Egg Color: Light Brown

Egg Size: Large

Classification: English

Comb Style: Single

Temperament: Exceptionally docile.

Broody: Sometimes

Colors: The original colors of black, white, buff, and blue are the most popular. Other colors are available and are still being developed.

PLYMOUTH ROCK: Known as "the chicken your grandma had", Plymouth Rocks originated in the United States and get their name from the town of Plymouth. After WWII, it became the most popular breed in America.

Size: 7 lbs. (female), 9 lbs. (male)

Number of eggs per week: Good

Classification: American

Egg Color: Brown

Egg Size: Large

Comb Style: Single

Temperament: Docile and friendly.

Broody: Yes. Make good mothers.

Colors: They come in several varieties, barred, buff and white being the most common. Other colors are partridge, silver laced, blue, and Columbian.

REDCAP: This bird sports a huge red comb, hence its name. Also known as the Derbyshire Redcap.
Size: 6 lbs. (female), 7 lbs. (male)
Number of eggs per week: Good
Egg Color: White
Egg Size: Medium
Classification: English
Comb Style: Rose
Temperament: Somewhat wild.
Broody: No
Color: Reddish brown to bluish-black.

RED STAR: This breed is a sex-link, meaning that it can be sexed based on its color immediately after hatching. Female chicks are buff or brown/red and male chicks are white. Red Stars are created by crossing a red hen with a White Rock, Silver Laced Wyandotte, Delaware, or Rhode Island White. Unlike many breeds, they will produce heavily through hot and cold weather. They sometimes go by the names Production Red, Golden Buff, Comet, Golden Comet, Golden Sex Link, and Isa Brown. Sex link chickens are not recommended as breeding stock since there is no way to know which characteristics they will pass along to their offspring.
Size: 5 lbs. (female), 6 lbs. (male)
Number of eggs per week: Excellent

Egg Color: Brown

Egg Size: Large to Extra Large

Classification: Not recognized

Comb Style: Single

Temperament: Easy going.

Broody: No

Color: Reddish brown with small areas of white sprinkled throughout.

RHODE ISLAND RED or WHITE: The official state bird of Rhode Island. It dates back to the mid 1840's, making it one of the oldest breeds in America.

Size: 6 lbs. (female), 8 lbs. (male)

Number of eggs per week: Excellent

Egg Color: Brown

Egg Size: Large

Classification: American

Comb Style: Single

Temperament: Good natured and docile.

Broody: No

Colors: Reddish-brown. There is also a White Rhode Island, though not as common.

SUSSEX: This breed was developed in the county of Sussex. Prior to the development of the Cornish Cross, the Sussex was the meat bird of choice in England.

Size: 7 lbs. (female), 9 lbs. (male)

Number of eggs per week: Good

Egg Color: Tinted to Light Brown

Egg Size: Medium

Classification: English

Comb Style: Single

Temperament: Calm, docile and curious.

Broody: Yes

Colors: Speckled, Red, Light

WELSUMMER (or WELSUMER): This breed takes its name from the village of Welsum, Holland. They lay dark brown eggs, often with speckles. Incidentally, the rooster on the Corn Flakes box was a Welsummer.

Size: 6 lbs. (female), 7 lbs. (male)

Number of eggs per week: Good

Egg Color: Brown

Egg Size: Large

Classification: Continental

Comb Style: Single

Temperament: Docile, intelligent and easy to handle.

Broody: Sometimes

Color: Red Partridge

WYANDOTTE: An American breed that is a favorite among backyard chickens keepers because of the large number of color possibilities.

Size: 6 lbs. (female), 8 lbs. (male)

Number of eggs per week: Good

Egg Color: Brown or tinted

Egg Size: Large

Classification: American

Comb Style: Rose

Temperament: Friendly and make good pets.

Broody: Sometimes

Colors: They come in seventeen colors. The most common being silver laced, golden laced, white, black, buff, partridge, silver penciled, Columbian, and blue.

EXHIBITION BREEDS

Back in the day, chickens were raised for either their eggs or their meat. Now, some chickens are raised purely for their beauty. Many of these show chickens were once kept for their eggs or meat, but have since been replaced by breeds that topped them in those categories. Fortunately, these birds did not die out when their usefulness ended. Their unique beauty landed them a new role as "runway models" in the chicken world. Some of them sport fancy headgear, feathered legs, streaming tail feathers, and fluffy beards. Others are not as showy but are still beautiful breeds for exhibition.

The following are some of the most popular exhibition breeds.

AMERAUCANA: Sometimes confused with Easter Eggers or Americanas. Unlike these mixed breed birds, Ameraucanas are a purebred breed. Be sure to check the spelling before you accidentally purchase an Americana thinking that it is an Ameraucana.
Size: 5 lbs. (female), 6 lbs. (male)
Number of eggs per week: Good
Egg Color: Green or Blue
Egg Size: Large

Classification: All Other

Comb Style: Pea

Temperament: Calm and not afraid of people.

Broody: Yes

Colors: Black, Blue, Blue-wheaten, Brown-red, Buff, Silver, Wheaten, White

ARAUCANA: Araucanas originated in Chile. They are sometimes confused with Easter Eggers, Americanas, and Ameraucanas, which are breeds that also lay colored eggs. The Araucana is different from these breeds because they have ear tufts, and no tail. Also known as the South American Rumpless.

Size: 4 lbs. (female), 5 lbs. (male)

Number of eggs per week: Good

Egg Color: Blue

Egg Size: Medium

Classification: All Other

Comb Style: Pea

Temperament: Calm

Broody: Yes

Colors: Black, White, Black Breasted Red, Blue, Buff, Silver

ANDALUSIAN: Sometimes called the Blue Andalusian, this breed originated in the Andalucia region of Spain. Oddly, when two blues are bred, the result is some whites and some blacks, making this breed rare except among poultry enthusiasts.

Size: 5 lbs. (female), 7 lbs. (male)

Number of eggs per week: Good

Egg Color: White

Egg Size: Large

Classification: Mediterranean

Comb Style: Single

Temperament: Flighty

Broody: No

Colors: The color recognized by the American Poultry Association is blue. They also can be black and mottled.

APPENZELLER: This breed originated in the Appenzell region of Switzerland. There are two types of Appenzellers – Spitzhauben and Barthuhner. The Spitzhauben is more popular in North America. These chickens sport a comical, yet interesting crest of feathers on their heads.

Size: 3 lbs. (female), 4 lbs. (male)

Number of eggs per week: Good

Egg Color: White

Egg Size: Medium

Classification: Not recognized

Comb Style: V-shaped

Temperament: Can be very friendly once trained.

Broody: No

Color: White with black spots.

BRAHMA: One of the larger breeds, this chicken is known as The Gentle Giant because of its exceptionally calm, friendly demeanor.

Size: 9 lbs. (female), 12 lbs. (male)

Number of eggs per week: Good

Egg Color: Brown

Egg Size: Large

Classification: Asiatic

Comb Style: Pea

Temperament: Extremely gentle and tame.

Broody: Yes

Colors: Light, Dark, Buff

CAMPINE: This breed originated in Belgium's Campine region. They are small bodied and are full of energy and character. These birds are fun to watch but don't especially like human contact.

Size: 4 lbs. (female), 6 lbs. (male)

Number of eggs per week: Good

Egg Color: White

Egg Size: Medium

Classification: Continental

Comb Style: Single

Temperament: Lively and sometimes almost wild acting.

Broody: No

Colors: Gold, Silver

COCHIN: These adorable balls of fluff are as friendly as they appear. They originated in China where they were known as the Shanghai. Very popular as pets or exhibition birds.

Size: 8 lbs. (female), 11 lbs. (male)

Number of eggs per week: Fair

Egg Color: Brown

Egg Size: Large

Classification: Asiatic

Comb Style: Single

Temperament: Calm, docile and sweet.

Broody: Yes

Colors: Buff, White, Black, Partridge

CREVECOEUR: This beautiful bird with a showy black crest gets its name from Crève-Coeur en Ange, a small town in Normandy, France. It is thought to be one of the oldest French breeds.

Size: 6 lbs. (female), 8 lbs. (male)

Number of eggs per week: Good

Egg Color: White

Egg Size: Medium

Classification: Continental

Comb Style: V-shaped

Temperament: Quiet and easy to handle.

Broody: No

Color: Black

DORKING: It is believed that the Dorking originated in Italy and dates back to the days of the Roman Empire. This makes it one of the oldest English breeds. What makes this bird unique is the fact that it has five toes rather than the standard four.

Size: 7 lbs. (female), 9 lbs. (male)

Number of eggs per week: Good

Egg Color: White

Egg Size: Large

Classification: English

Comb Style: Rose and Single

Temperament: Quiet and calm.

Broody: Yes

Colors: White, Dark, Silver Grey, Cuckoo, Red (extremely rare)

FAVEROLLE: This breed is strangely beautiful with its muffs, beard and feathered legs. It also has five toes as opposed to the typical four.

Size: 6 lbs. (female), 8 lbs. (male)

Number of eggs per week: Good

Egg Color: Creamy to light brown

Egg Size: Medium

Classification: Continental

Comb Style: Single

Temperament: Shy and sweet.

Broody: Yes

Colors: Salmon, White

HOUDAN: This is an old breed native to France. They are known for their large puffy crests and beards. Like the Dorking, they have five toes rather than the standard four.

Size: 6 lbs. (female), 8 lbs. (male)

Number of eggs per week: Fair

Egg Color: White

Egg Size: Small

Classification: Continental

Comb Style: V-shaped

Temperament: Docile and easy to handle.

Broody: Yes

Colors: White, Mottled

LANGSHAN: The Langshan is an endangered breed that originated in China. These tall, large birds are filled with poise and grace. Most have feathered feet, though some do not.

Size: 7 lbs. (female), 9 lbs. (male)

Number of eggs per week: Fair

Egg Color: Brown

Egg Size: Large

Classification: Asiatic

Comb Style: Single

Temperament: Not as calm as most large breeds.

Broody: Yes

Colors: Black, White, Blue

NAKED NECK: As its name implies, this odd looking chicken doesn't have feathers on its neck. In fact, it has almost half the feathers of other breeds its size. Also known as a Turken.

Size: 6 lbs. (female), 8 lbs. (male)

Number of eggs per week: Good

Egg Color: Tinted to Light Brown

Egg Size: Medium

Classification: All Other

Comb Style: Single

Temperament: Calm, active, yet easy to handle.

Broody: Yes

Colors: Black, white and red are recognized by the American Poultry Association. Other varieties are blue, cuckoo, and barred.

POLISH: This breed is known for its comical bouffant crest feathers that give it a Phyllis Diller look. Comes in bearded and beardless varieties.

Size: 4 lbs. (female), 6 lbs. (male)

Number of eggs per week: Good

Egg Color: White

Egg Size: Medium

Classification: Continental

Comb Style: V-Shaped

Temperament: Somewhat flighty and often on the bottom of the pecking order.

Broody: No

Colors: Black, White, Golden, Silver, Buff Laced

SICILIAN BUTTERCUP: This bird comes from Sicily and wears a cup shaped comb.

Size: 5 lbs. (female), 6 lbs. (male)

Number of eggs per week: Good

Egg Color: White

Egg Size: Medium

Classification: Mediterranean

Comb Style: Buttercup

Temperament: Flighty

Broody: No

Color: Buff with black spots.

SILKIE: These pretty little birds are one of the most popular choices for children and adults alike. They are "lap chickens" and are known for their soft, fluffy feathers that resemble fur. They come in bearded and beardless varieties. One of the few breeds with five toes rather than four. This breed is a true bantam, meaning that it does not have a standard size counterpart.

Size: 16 oz. (female), 36 oz. (male)

Number of eggs per week: Fair

Egg Color: Tinted

Egg Size: Small

Classification: All Other Combs, Feather Legged, True Bantam

Comb Style: Walnut

Temperament: Very tame and love to be around people.

Broody: Yes

Colors: Black, White, Blue, Buff, Partridge, Gray

SPANISH: An aristocrat in the chicken world, this breed is known for its stunning white face and earlobes against greenish, black plumage. Also known as White-Faced Black Spanish, Spanish White Ear, or Clown Face

Size: 6 lbs. (female), 8 lbs. (male)

Number of eggs per week: Good

Egg Color: White

Egg Size: Large

Classification: Mediterranean

Comb Style: Single

Temperament: Flighty

Broody: No

Color: Buff with black spots.

SULTAN: These showy birds have a cascade of feathers on top of their heads, muffs, beards, feathered feet, and five toes.

Size: 4 lbs. (female), 6 lbs. (male)

Number of eggs per week: Fair

Egg Color: White

Egg Size: Small

Classification: All Other

Comb Style: V-Shaped

Temperament: Calm and easy to handle.

Broody: No

Color: White

YOKOHAMA: These fancy birds have unusually, long, graceful tail feathers, making it necessary to give them high perches and special cages to keep them tidy.

Size: 3 lbs. (female), 4 lbs. (male)

Number of eggs per week: Poor

Egg Color: Tinted

Egg Size: Small

Classification: All Other

Comb Style: Walnut

Temperament: Docile but not recommended for mixed flocks.

Broody: No

Colors: White, Red Shouldered and White

BANTAMS

Nothing is as cute as a miniature chicken! If you're looking for a pet chicken, bantams (or banties as they are sometimes called) are an excellent choice. They are approximately ¼ - ½ the size of their standard size counterparts. Accordingly, their eggs are much smaller and they lay fewer of them. Most bantams are merely miniature versions of standard size chickens that have been developed using selective breeding. There are really only a few true bantams. That is, bantams that don't originate from a standard size breed. If space is at a premium, these little birds can get by with less real estate than standard size birds.

The following are some of the most popular bantam breeds.

AMERAUCANA: Sometimes confused with Easter Eggers or Americanas. Unlike these mixed breed birds, Ameraucanas are a purebred breed. Be sure to check the spelling before you accidentally purchase an Americana thinking that it is an Ameraucana.
Size: 26 oz. (female), 30 oz. (male)
Number of eggs per week: Good
Egg Color: Green or Blue

Egg Size: Small

Classification: All Other Clean Legged Bantam

Temperament: Calm and not afraid of people.

Broody: Yes

Colors: Black, Blue, Blue-wheaten, Brown-red, Buff, Silver, Wheaten, White

ANCONA: This breed gets its name from its original breeding place, Ancona, Italy. It arrived in the United States in the late 1800's and quickly became a popular breed.

Size: 22 oz. (female), 26 oz. (male)

Number of eggs per week: Excellent

Egg Color: White

Egg Size: Small

Classification: Single Comb, Clean Legged, Bantam

Temperament: Have some wild tendencies and are a bit flighty.

Broody: No

Color: Black with white mottling.

ANDALUSIAN: Sometimes called the Blue Andalusian, this breed originated in the Andalucia region of Spain. Oddly, when two blues are bred, the result is some whites and some blacks, making this breed rare except among poultry enthusiasts.

Size: 24 oz. (female), 28 oz. (male)

Number of eggs per week: Good

Egg Color: White

Egg Size: Small

Classification: Single Comb, Clean Legged, Bantam

Temperament: Flighty

Broody: No

Colors: The color recognized by the American Poultry Association is blue. They also can be black and mottled.

ARAUCANA: Araucanas originated in Chile. They are sometimes confused with Easter Eggers, Americanas, and Ameraucanas, which are breeds that also lay colored eggs. The Araucana is different from these breeds because they have ear tufts, and no tail. Also known as the South American Rumpless.

Size: 24 oz. (female), 26 oz. (male)

Number of eggs per week: Good

Egg Color: Blue

Egg Size: Small

Classification: All Other Combs, Clean Legged, Bantam

Temperament: Calm

Broody: Yes

Colors: Black, White, Black Breasted Red, Blue, Buff, Silver

AUSTRALORP: This breed originated in Australia, as the name suggests, and was developed from England's Black Orpington. In the 1920's, the breed set a world record for most eggs laid in a year (364). Size: 26 oz. (female), 30 oz. (male)

Number of eggs per week: Excellent

Egg Color: Brown

Egg Size: Small

Classification: Single Comb, Clean Legged, Bantam

Temperament: Sweet, good natured chickens that make excellent pets and are good around children. They do not mind being handled and enjoy being petted.

Broody: Sometimes

Color: Shiny black feathers with iridescent green and purple highlights that glisten in sunlight.

BEARDED D'ANVERS: This true bantam (meaning it has no standard size counterpart) comes from Belgium. Also known as the Antwerp Belgian, Belgian Bearded d'Anvers, and Barbu d'Anvers. Kept mainly as a pet or for showing.

Size: 22 oz. (female), 26 oz. (male)

Number of eggs per week: Fair

Egg Color: White

Egg Size: Small

Classification: Rose Comb, Clean Legged, True Bantam

Temperament: Friendly

Broody: Yes

Colors: Most common colors are quail, porcelain, black, blue, buff, cuckoo, mille fleur, white, and mottled.

BEARDED D'UCCLE: The d'Uccle is a feather legged bird comes from the town of Uccle on the outskirts of Brussels, Belgium. Also known as the Belgian d'Uccle, Barbu d'Uccle or Mille Fleur.

Size: 22 oz. (female), 26 oz. (male)

Number of eggs per week: Fair

Egg Color: White

Egg Size: Small

Classification: Single Comb, Feather Legged, True Bantam

Temperament: Very calm.

Broody: Yes

Colors: Most common colors are mille fleur, porcelain, black, buff, white, blue mottled, splash, lavender, and golden neck.

BOOTED: Also known as Sablepoot, this is an old bantam breed from the Netherlands. They have an upright carriage and striking plumage.

Size: 22 oz. (female), 26 oz. (male)

Number of eggs per week: Fair

Egg Color: White

Egg Size: Small

Classification: Single Comb, Feather Legged, True Bantam

Temperament: Calm and docile.

Broody: Yes

Colors: Black, Blue, Buff, Mille Fleur, Porcelain, White, Mottled

BRAHMA: One of the larger breeds, this chicken is known as The Gentle Giant because of its exceptionally calm, friendly demeanor.

Size: 34 oz. (female), 38 oz. (male)

Number of eggs per week: Good

Egg Color: Brown

Egg Size: Small

Classification: Pea Comb, Feather Legged, Bantam

Temperament: Extremely gentle and tame.

Broody: Yes

Colors: Light, Dark, Buff

CAMPINE: This breed originated in Belgium's Campine region. They are small bodied and are full of energy and character. These birds are fun to watch but don't especially like human contact.
Size: 22 oz. (female), 26 oz. (male)
Number of eggs per week: Good
Egg Color: White
Egg Size: Small
Classification: Single Comb, Clean Legged, Bantam
Temperament: Lively and sometimes almost wild acting.
Broody: No
Colors: Gold, Silver

CATALANA: The Catalana was developed in the district of Catalonia Spain, which is near Barcelona. The breed is more popular in South American and Spain than in the United States.
Size: 28 oz. (female), 32 oz. (male)
Number of eggs per week: Good
Egg Color: White to tinted
Egg Size: Small
Classification: Single Comb, Clean Legged, Bantam
Temperament: Active and avoids people.
Broody: No
Color: Buff

CHANTECLER: Known as Canada's breed, the Chantecler was developed by Brother Wilfred Chatalain of the Oka Agricultural Institute in Quebec. It is a bit chubby and a great choice for those in a cold climate.
Size: 30 oz. (female), 34 oz. (male)

Number of eggs per week: Good

Egg Color: Brown

Egg Size: Small

Classification: All Other Combs, Clean Legged, Bantam

Temperament: Quiet and easy to handle.

Broody: Yes

Colors: White, Buff, Partridge

COCHIN: These adorable balls of fluff are as friendly as they appear. They originated in China where they were known as the Shanghai. Very popular as pets or exhibition birds.

Size: 28 oz. (female), 32 oz. (male)

Number of eggs per week: Fair

Egg Color: Brown

Egg Size: Large

Classification: Single Comb, Feather Legged, Bantam

Temperament: Calm, docile and sweet.

Broody: Yes

Colors: Buff, White, Black, Partridge

CORNISH: These stocky birds originated in Cornwall, England. If you buy chicken from a supermarket, most likely it came from Cornish birds that were crossed with a White Plymouth Rock. Also known as Indian Game.

Size: 36 oz. (female), 44 oz. (male)

Number of eggs per week: Poor

Egg Color: Light Brown

Egg Size: Small

Classification: All Other Combs, Clean Legged, Bantam

Temperament: Slow, docile and noisy.

Broody: No

Colors: White, Dark, White Laced, Red, Buff

CREVECOEUR: This beautiful bird with a showy black crest gets its name from Crève-Coeur en Ange, a small town in Normandy, France. It is thought to be one of the oldest French breeds.

Size: 26 oz. (female), 30 oz. (male)

Number of eggs per week: Good

Egg Color: White

Egg Size: Small

Classification: All Other Combs, Clean Legged, Bantam

Temperament: Quiet and easy to handle.

Broody: No

Color: Black

DELAWARE: This breed originates from Delaware. It was once quite common, but is now endangered.

Size: 30 oz. (female), 34 oz. (male)

Number of eggs per week: Good

Egg Color: Brown

Egg Size: Small

Classification: Single Comb, Clean Legged, Bantam

Temperament: Friendly and calm.

Broody: Yes

Color: White body with light black barring on the hackle, wings and tail.

DOMINQUE: This heritage breed is sometimes confused with a Barred Rock because they both have a barred pattern. The difference between the two breeds is that the Dominique has a rose comb while the Barred Rock has a single comb. Also goes by the name Dominiker.

Size: 24 oz. (female), 28 oz. (male)

Number of eggs per week: Good

Egg Color: Brown

Egg Size: Small

Classification: Rose Comb, Clean Legged, Bantam

Temperament: Calm

Broody: Yes

Colors: Barred Black/White

DORKING: It is believed that the Dorking originated in Italy and dates back to the days of the Roman Empire. This makes it one of the oldest English breeds. What makes this bird unique is the fact that it has five toes rather than the standard four.

Size: 32 oz. (female), 36 oz. (male)

Number of eggs per week: Good

Egg Color: White

Egg Size: Small

Classification: Single Comb, Clean Legged, Bantam

Temperament: Quiet and calm.

Broody: Yes

Colors: White, Dark, Silver Grey, Cuckoo, Red (extremely rare)

DUTCH: The Dutch was developed in the Netherlands and is known as the smallest of the bantams. They lay a fair number of eggs in spite of their small size.

Size: 20 oz. (female), 21 oz. (male)

Number of eggs per week: Fair

Egg Color: Tinted

Egg Size: Small

Classification: Single Comb, Clean Legged, True Bantam

Temperament: Friendly but somewhat flighty.

Broody: Yes

Colors: Most common colors are light brown, white, black, blue, light brown, silver

FAVEROLLE: This breed is strangely beautiful with its muffs, beard and feathered legs. It also has five toes as opposed to the typical four.

Size: 26 oz. (female), 30 oz. (male)

Number of eggs per week: Good

Egg Color: Creamy to light brown

Egg Size: Small

Classification: All Other Combs, Clean Legged, Bantam

Temperament: Shy and sweet.

Broody: Yes

Colors: Salmon, White

HAMBURG: The Hamburg originated hundreds of years ago in Holland. These active birds are known for their economical eating.

Size: 22 oz. (female), 26 oz. (male)

Number of eggs per week: Good

Egg Color: White

Egg Size: Small

Classification: Rose Comb, Clean Legged, Bantam

Temperament: Flighty and avoid human contact.

Broody: No

Colors: Silver-Spangled, Golden-Spangled, Golden-Penciled, Silver-Penciled, White, Black

HOLLAND: The Holland was NOT developed in Holland. In fact, it was created in New Jersey. One of the breeds used in its development, however, was imported from Holland.

Size: 6 lbs. (female), 8 lbs. (male)

Number of eggs per week: Good

Egg Color: White

Egg Size: Small

Classification: Single Comb, Clean Legged, Bantam

Temperament: Calm and even tempered.

Broody: Sometimes

Colors: White, Barred

HOUDAN: This is an old breed native to France. They are known for their large puffy crests and beards. Like the Dorking, they have five toes rather than the standard four.

Size: 30 oz. (female), 34 oz. (male)

Number of eggs per week: Fair

Egg Color: White

Egg Size: Small

Classification: All Other Combs, Clean Legged, Bantam

Temperament: Docile and easy to handle.

Broody: Yes

Colors: White, Mottled

JAPANESE: These birds have extremely short legs and upright tails that often reach over their heads. Also known as Chabo, which means dwarf.

Size: 22 oz. (female), 26 oz. (male)

Number of eggs per week: Poor

Egg Color: Brown

Egg Size: Small

Classification: Single Comb, Clean Legged, True Bantam

Temperament: Docile and friendly.

Broody: Yes

Colors: Most common colors are black, white, black tailed, birchen, and mottled.

JAVA: Now a critically endangered breed, the Java is one of America's oldest breeds and was instrumental in developing popular breeds such as the Plymouth Rock and Rhode Island Red, to name a few.

Size: 32 oz. (female), 36 oz. (male)

Number of eggs per week: Fair

Egg Color: Brown

Egg Size: Medium

Classification: Single Comb, Clean Legged, Bantam

Temperament: Calm

Broody: Yes

Colors: Black, White, Mottled

JERSEY GIANT: The standard size version of the Jersey Giant is the largest chicken breed available. The bantam version is also quite large among bantams. As its name implies, it was developed in New Jersey.

Size: 34 oz. (female), 38oz. (male)

Number of eggs per week: Good

Egg Color: Brown

Egg Size: Small

Classification: Single Comb, Clean Legged, Bantam

Temperament: Gentle

Broody: Sometimes

Colors: Black, White

LA FLECHE: This French breed is also known as the "Devil Bird" because its V-shaped comb resembles horns.

Size: 26 oz. (female), 30 oz. (male)

Number of eggs per week: Good

Egg Color: White

Egg Size: Small

Classification: All Other Combs, Clean Legged, Bantam

Temperament: Does not like human contact and acts slightly wild.

Broody: No

Colors: Its official color is black, though it also comes in blue, white, and cuckoo.

LAKENVELDER: This rare variety was bred in the early 1800's in Germany and Holland. It has distinct black and white markings, making it a beautiful specimen.

Size: 20 oz. (female), 24 oz. (male)

Number of eggs per week: Good

Egg Color: White

Egg Size: Small

Classification: Single Comb, Clean Legged, Bantam

Temperament: Flighty and avoids human contact.

Broody: No

Colors: Black and White pattern

LANGSHAN: The Langshan is an endangered breed that originated in China. These tall, large birds are filled with poise and grace. Most have feathered feet, though some do not.

Size: 32 oz. (female), 36 oz. (male)

Number of eggs per week: Fair

Egg Color: Brown

Egg Size: Small

Classification: Single Comb, Feather Legged, Bantam

Temperament: Calm

Broody: Yes

Colors: Black, White, Blue

LEGHORN: Because they are prolific layers, most commercially produced eggs come from Leghorns. They originated in Italy and get their name from Livorno (also known as Leghorn).

Size: 20 oz. (female), 24 oz. (male)

Number of eggs per week: Excellent

Egg Color: White

Egg Size: Small

Classification: Single Comb, Clean Legged, Bantam

Temperament: Slightly nervous and can be flighty. Not the best choice if you are looking for a bird you can interact with easily. Leghorns are used as a cross in many modern breeds and when bred with a calmer bird, the temperament of their offspring improves.

Broody: No

Colors: Most commonly brown or white. Buff, black, silver, and other colors are available, though rare.

MINORCA: This breed gets its name from the Island of Minorca off the coast of Spain. It is sometimes called the "Red Faced Black Chicken" because of its red face and large red wattle and comb.

Size: 26 oz. (female), 32 oz. (male)

Number of eggs per week: Excellent

Egg Color: White

Egg Size: Small

Classification: Single Comb, Clean Legged, Bantam

Temperament: Avoids human contact.

Broody: No

Colors: Black, White, Buff

NAKED NECK: As its name implies, this odd looking chicken doesn't have feathers on its neck. In fact, it has almost half the feathers of other breeds its size. Also known as a Turken.

Size: 30 oz. (female), 34 oz. (male)

Number of eggs per week: Good

Egg Color: Tinted to Light Brown

Egg Size: Small

Classification: Single Comb, Clean Legged, Bantam

Temperament: Calm, active, yet easy to handle.

Broody: Yes

Colors: Black, white and red are recognized by the American Poultry Association. Other varieties are blue, cuckoo, or barred.

NEW HAMPSHIRE: This breed was developed from the Rhode Island Red. Also known as New Hampshire Red.

Size: 30 oz. (female), 34 oz. (male)

Number of eggs per week: Fair

Egg Color: Brown

Egg Size: Small

Classification: Single Comb, Clean Legged, Bantam

Temperament: Docile, friendly and does not mind being handled.

Broody: Yes

Color: Light Reddish Brown

ORPINGTON: One of the smartest breeds. Believe it or not, some owners claim they are able to teach their Orpington tricks.

Size: 34 oz. (female), 38 oz. (male)

Number of eggs per week: Good

Egg Color: Light Brown

Egg Size: Small

Classification: Single Comb, Clean Legged, Bantam

Temperament: Exceptionally docile.

Broody: Sometimes

Colors: The original colors of black, white, buff, and blue are the most popular. Other colors are available and are still being developed.

PHOENIX: This ancient Japanese breed often require special cages and high perches to keep their long tail feathers clean. They were once kept in the imperial gardens and prized for their striking tail feathers.

Size: 24 oz. (female), 26 oz. (male)

Number of eggs per week: Poor

Egg Color: Tinted

Egg Size: Small

Classification: Single Comb, Clean Legged, Bantam

Temperament: Docile

Broody: No

Colors: Partridge, Silver Duckwing, White

PLYMOUTH ROCK: Known as "the chicken your grandma had", Plymouth Rocks originated in the United States and get their name from the town of Plymouth. After WWII, they became the most popular breed in America.

Size: 36 oz. (female), 44 oz. (male)

Number of eggs per week: Good

Classification: Single Comb, Clean Legged, Bantam

Egg Color: Brown

Egg Size: Small

Comb Style: Single

Temperament: Docile and friendly.

Broody: Yes. Make good mothers.

Colors: They come in several varieties, barred (black with white "barring"), buff and white being

the most common. Other colors are partridge, silver laced, blue, and Columbian.

POLISH: This breed is known for its comical bouffant crest feathers that give it a Phyllis Diller look. It comes in bearded and beardless varieties.

Size: 4 lbs. (female), 6 lbs. (male)

Number of eggs per week: Good

Egg Color: White

Egg Size: Small

Classification: All Other Combs, Clean Legged, Bantam

Temperament: Somewhat flighty and often on the bottom of the pecking order.

Broody: No

Colors: Black, White, Golden, Silver, Buff Laced

REDCAP: The Redcap sports a huge red comb, hence its name. Also known as the Derbyshire Redcap.

Size: 26 oz. (female), 30 oz. (male)

Number of eggs per week: Good

Egg Color: White

Egg Size: Small

Classification: Rose Comb, Clean Legged, Bantam

Temperament: Somewhat wild.

Broody: No

Color: Reddish brown to bluish-black.

RHODE ISLAND RED or WHITE: The official state bird of Rhode Island. It dates back to the mid 1840's, making it one of the oldest breeds in America.

Size: 30 oz. (female), 34 oz. (male)

Number of eggs per week: Excellent

Egg Color: Brown

Egg Size: Small

Classification: Single Comb, Clean Legged, Bantam

Temperament: Good natured and docile.

Broody: No

Colors: Reddish-brown. There is also a White Rhode Island, though not as common.

ROSECOMB: One of the most popular bantam show breeds, these birds got their name because of their unusually large rose combs. They are not especially hardy and are not recommended for first time chicken owners.

Size: 22 oz. (female), 26 oz. (male)

Number of eggs per week: Poor

Egg Color: White

Egg Size: Small

Classification: Rose Comb, Clean Legged, Bantam

Temperament: Docile

Broody: No

Colors: Recognized colors are black, white and blue.

SEBRIGHT: This breed is unique because it is the only breed that is "hen feathered", meaning that the males have the same feathering as the females. With most other breeds, males have pointed hackle and saddle feathers.

Size: 20 oz. (female), 22 oz. (male)

Number of eggs per week: Poor

Egg Color: White

Egg Size: Small

Classification: Single Comb, Clean Legged, True Bantam

Temperament: Active

Broody: No
Colors: Silver, Gold

SILKIE: These pretty little birds are one of the most popular choices for children and adults alike. They are "lap chickens" and are known for their soft, fluffy feathers that resemble fur. They come in bearded and beardless varieties. One of the few breeds with five toes rather than four. This breed is a true bantam, meaning that it does not have a standard size counterpart.
Size: 16 oz. (female), 36 oz. (male)
Number of eggs per week: Fair
Egg Color: Tinted
Egg Size: Small
Classification: All Other Combs, Feather Legged, True Bantam
Temperament: Very tame and love to be around people.
Broody: Yes
Colors: Black, White, Blue, Buff, Partridge, Gray

SPANISH: An aristocrat in the chicken world, this breed is known for its stunning white face and earlobes against greenish, black plumage. Also known as White-Faced Black Spanish, Spanish White Ear, or Clown Face
Size: 26 oz. (female), 30 oz. (male)
Number of eggs per week: Good
Egg Color: White
Egg Size: Small
Classification: Single Comb, Clean Legged, Bantam
Temperament: Flighty
Broody: No
Color: Buff with black spots.

SULTAN: These showy birds have a cascade of feathers on top of their heads, muffs, beards, feathered feet, and five toes.

Size: 22 oz. (female), 26 oz. (male)

Number of eggs per week: Fair

Egg Color: White

Egg Size: Small

Classification: All Other Combs, Feather Legged, Bantam

Temperament: Calm and easy to handle.

Broody: No

Color: White

SUMATRA: This bird comes from the island of Sumatra off southeast Asia and is thought to be related to the jungle fowl of the Far East. It sports a long, graceful tail that can grow as long as four feet on roosters.

Size: 22 oz. (female), 24 oz. (male)

Number of eggs per week: Fair

Egg Color: White

Egg Size: Small

Classification: All Other Combs, Clean Legged, Bantam

Temperament: Can be quite wild and hard to tame.

Broody: Yes

Colors: Black, Blue

SUSSEX: This breed was developed in the county of Sussex. Prior to the development of the Cornish Cross, the Sussex was the meat bird of choice in England.

Size: 32 oz. (female), 36 oz. (male)

Number of eggs per week: Fair

Egg Color: Tinted to Light Brown

Egg Size: Small

Classification: Single Comb, Clean Legged, Bantam

Temperament: Calm, docile and curious.

Broody: Yes

Colors: Speckled, Red, Light

WYANDOTTE: An American breed that is a favorite among backyard chickens keepers because of the large number of color possibilities.

Size: 26 oz. (female), 30 oz. (male)

Number of eggs per week: Good

Egg Color: Brown or tinted

Egg Size: Small

Classification: Rose Comb, Clean Legged, Bantam

Temperament: Friendly and make good pets.

Broody: Sometimes

Colors: They come in seventeen colors. The most common being Silver Laced, Golden Laced, White, Black, Buff, Partridge, Silver Penciled, Columbian, and Blue.

YOKOHAMA: These fancy birds have unusually, long, graceful tail feathers, making it necessary to give them high perches and special cages to keep them tidy.

Size: 22 oz. (female), 26 oz. (male)

Number of eggs per week: Poor

Egg Color: Tinted

Egg Size: Small

Classification: All Other Combs, Clean Legged, Bantam

Temperament: Docile but not recommended for mixed flocks.

Broody: No

Colors: White, Red Shouldered and White

CLIMATE CONSIDERATIONS - COLD TOLERANT BREEDS

It's important to choose a breed that will do well in your climate. Some are especially suited for cold weather, some for hot weather, and some for both.

Let's start with breeds that do well in cold climates. These birds typically have smaller combs, which lessens their risk for frostbite. They are also more heavily feathered. Though, there are a few exceptions to this rule. For example, the Naked Neck has half the feathers of a typical chicken and does well in cold climates. Go figure!

APPENZELLER: This breed originated in the Appenzell region of Switzerland. There are two types of Appenzellers – Spitzhauben and Barthuhner. The Spitzhauben is more popular in North America. These chickens sport a comical, yet interesting crest of feathers on their heads.
Size: 3 lbs. (female), 4 lbs. (male)
Number of eggs per week: Good
Egg Color: White
Egg Size: Medium

Classification: Not recognized

Comb Style: V-shaped

Temperament: Can be very friendly once trained.

Broody: No

Color: White with black spots.

ARAUCANA: Araucanas originated in Chile. They are sometimes confused with Easter Eggers, Americanas, and Ameraucanas, which are breeds that also lay colored eggs. The Araucana is different from these breeds because they have ear tufts, and no tail. Also known as the South American Rumpless.

Size: 4 lbs. (female), 5 lbs. (male)

Number of eggs per week: Fair

Egg Color: Blue

Egg Size: Medium

Classification: All Other

Comb Style: Pea

Temperament: Calm

Broody: Yes

Colors: Black, White, Black Breasted Red, Blue, Buff, Silver

AUSTRALORP: This breed originated in Australia, as the name suggests, and was developed from England's Black Orpington. In the 1920's, the breed set a world record for most eggs laid in a year (364). Size: 6 lbs. (female), 8 lbs. (male)

Number of eggs per week: Excellent

Egg Color: Brown

Egg Size: Large

Classification: English

Comb Style: Single

Temperament: Sweet, good natured chickens that make excellent pets and are good around children. They do not mind being handled and enjoy being petted.

Broody: Can be broody. Good mother.

Color: Shiny black feathers with iridescent green and purple highlights that glisten in sunlight.

BARNEVELDER: Known for its dark, chocolate colored eggs, the Barnevelder originated in the Dutch town of Barneveld. Over the years, breeders have not concentrated on egg color and their dark brown eggs are not as dark as they once were.

Size: 6 lbs. (female), 7 lbs. (male)

Number of eggs per week: Good

Egg Color: Dark Brown

Egg Size: Large

Classification: Continental

Comb Style: Single

Temperament: Lively and friendly.

Broody: Sometimes

Colors: Double-laced Partridge, Blue-laced, White, Black

BRAHMA: One of the larger breeds, this chicken is known as The Gentle Giant because of its exceptionally calm, friendly demeanor.

Size: 9 lbs. (female), 12 lbs. (male)

Number of eggs per week: Good

Egg Color: Brown

Egg Size: Large

Classification: Asiatic

Comb Style: Pea

Temperament: Extremely gentle and tame.

Broody: Yes

Colors: Light, Dark, Buff

BUCKEYE: The Buckeye is the only American breed to be developed by a woman. Nettie Metcalf of Warren, Ohio, developed these winter-hardy layers in late 19th century. The Buckeye is a pea combed variety of the Rhode Island Red, and happens to be the only pea combed breed of American origin. As odd as it sounds, they are known for being good mousers.

Size: 5 lbs. (female), 9 lbs. (male)

Number of eggs per week: Good

Egg Color: Brown

Egg Size: Large

Classification: American

Comb Style: Pea

Temperament: Calm, friendly and easy to handle.

Broody: Sometimes

Color: Deep Brown

CALIFORNIA GRAY: Cross between a White Leghorn and a Barred Plymouth Rock that was developed in California in the 1930's.

Size: 4 lbs. (female), 5 lbs. (male)

Number of eggs per week: Good

Egg Color: White

Egg Size: Large

Classification: Not recognized

Comb Style: Single

Temperament: Docile and can be held.

Broody: No

Color: Barred Gray/White

CALIFORNIA WHITE: Cross between a White Leghorn hen and a California Gray rooster.

Size: 5 lbs. (female), 7 lbs. (male)

Number of eggs per week: Excellent

Egg Color: White

Egg Size: Large

Classification: Not recognized

Comb Style: Single

Temperament: Quiet and easy to handle.

Broody: No

Color: White

CAMPINE: This breed originated in Belgium's Campine region. They are small bodied and are full of energy and character. These birds are fun to watch but don't especially like human contact.

Size: 4 lbs. (female), 6 lbs. (male)

Number of eggs per week: Good

Egg Color: White

Egg Size: Medium

Classification: Continental

Comb Style: Single

Temperament: Lively and sometimes almost wild acting.

Broody: No

Colors: Gold, Silver

CHANTECLER: Known as Canada's breed, the Chantecler was developed by Brother Wilfred Chatalain of the Oka Agricultural Institute in Quebec. It is a bit chubby and a great choice for those in a cold climate.
Size: 6 lbs. (female), 8 lbs. (male)
Number of eggs per week: Good
Egg Color: Brown
Egg Size: Large
Classification: American
Comb Style: Cushion
Temperament: Quiet and easy to handle.
Broody: Yes
Colors: White, Buff, Partridge

COCHIN: These adorable balls of fluff are as friendly as they appear. They originated in China where they were known as the Shanghai. Very popular as pets or exhibition birds.
Size: 8 lbs. (female), 11 lbs. (male)
Number of eggs per week: Fair
Egg Color: Brown
Egg Size: Large
Classification: Asiatic
Comb Style: Single
Temperament: Calm, docile and sweet.
Broody: Yes
Colors: Buff, White, Black, Partridge

CORNISH: These stocky birds originated in Cornwall, England. If you buy chicken from a supermarket, most likely it came from Cornish birds that were crossed with a White Plymouth Rock. Also known as Indian Game.

Size: 8 lbs. (female), 10 lbs. (male)

Number of eggs per week: Poor

Egg Color: Light Brown

Egg Size: Small

Classification: English

Comb Style: Pea

Temperament: Slow, docile and noisy.

Broody: No

Colors: White, Dark, White Laced, Red, Buff

CORNISH CROSS (Cornish X Rock): These birds are cross between a white Cornish and a white Plymouth Rock. Due to their rapid growth and efficient use of feed, the Cornish Cross is the industry standard for meat production. They do not come without problems, however. Their fast growth subjects them to foot and heart issues. Not recommended for altitudes above 5000 feet. Also called Cornish/Rocks.

Size: 3 lbs. (female), 4 lbs. (male)

Number of eggs per week: Poor

Egg Color: Brown

Egg Size: Small

Classification: Not recognized

Comb Style: Pea

Temperament: Slow and lack energy. Sometimes they even eat sitting down.

Broody: No

Color: White

DELAWARE: This breed originates from Delaware. It was once quite common, but is now endangered.
Size: 6 lbs. (female), 8 lbs. (male)
Number of eggs per week: Good
Egg Color: Brown
Egg Size: Large
Classification: American
Comb Style: Single
Temperament: Friendly and calm.
Broody: Yes
Color: White body with light black barring on the hackle, wings and tail.

DOMINQUE: This heritage breed is sometimes confused with a Barred Rock because they both have a barred pattern. The difference between the two breeds is that the Dominique has a rose comb while the Barred Rock has a single comb. Also goes by the name Dominiker.
Size: 5 lbs. (female), 7 lbs. (male)
Number of eggs per week: Good
Egg Color: Brown
Egg Size: Medium
Classification: American
Comb Style: Rose
Temperament: Calm.
Broody: Yes
Color: Barred Black/White

DORKING: It is believed that the Dorking originated in Italy and dates back to the days of the Roman Empire. This makes it one of the oldest English breeds. What makes this bird unique is the fact that it has five toes rather than the standard four.

Size: 7 lbs. (female), 9 lbs. (male)

Number of eggs per week: Good

Egg Color: White

Egg Size: Large

Classification: English

Comb Style: Rose and Single

Temperament: Quiet and calm.

Broody: Yes

Colors: White, Dark, Silver Grey, Cuckoo, Red (extremely rare)

FAVEROLLE: This breed is strangely beautiful with its muffs, beard and feathered legs. It also has five toes as opposed to the typical four.

Size: 6 lbs. (female), 8 lbs. (male)

Number of eggs per week: Good

Egg Color: Creamy to light brown

Egg Size: Medium

Classification: Continental

Comb Style: Single

Temperament: Shy and sweet.

Broody: Yes

Colors: Salmon, White

HOLLAND: This breed was NOT developed in Holland. In fact, it was created in New Jersey. One of the breeds used in its development, however, was imported from Holland.

Size: 6 lbs. (female), 8 lbs. (male)

Number of eggs per week: Good

Egg Color: White

Egg Size: Large

Classification: American

Comb Style: Single

Temperament: Calm and even tempered.

Broody: Sometimes

Colors: White, Barred

JAVA: Now a critically endangered breed, the Java is one of America's oldest breeds and was instrumental in developing popular breeds such as the Plymouth Rock and Rhode Island Red, to name a few.

Size: 7 lbs. (female), 9 lbs. (male)

Number of eggs per week: Fair

Egg Color: Brown

Egg Size: Medium

Classification: American

Comb Style: Single

Temperament: Calm

Broody: Yes

Colors: Black, White, Mottled

JERSEY GIANT: The Jersey Giant is the largest chicken breed available. As its name implies, it was developed in New Jersey.

Size: 10 lbs. (female), 13 lbs. (male)

Number of eggs per week: Good

Egg Color: Brown

Egg Size: Extra Large

Classification: American

Comb Style: Single

Temperament: Gentle

Broody: Sometimes

Colors: Black, White

LANGSHAN: The Langshan is an endangered breed that originated in China. These tall, large birds are filled with poise and grace. Most have feathered feet, though some do not.

Size: 7 lbs. (female), 9 lbs. (male)

Number of eggs per week: Fair

Egg Color: Brown

Egg Size: Large

Classification: Asiatic

Comb Style: Single

Temperament: Not as calm as most large breeds.

Broody: Yes

Colors: Black, White, Blue

LA FLECHE: This French breed is also known as the "Devil Bird" because its V-shaped comb resembles horns.

Size: 6 lbs. (female), 8 lbs. (male)

Number of eggs per week: Good

Egg Color: White

Egg Size: Large

Classification: Continental

Comb Style: V-Shaped

Temperament: Does not like human contact and acts slightly wild.

Broody: No

Colors: Its official color is black, though it also comes in blue, white, and cuckoo.

LEGHORN: Because they are prolific layers, most commercially produced eggs come from Leghorns. They originated in Italy and get their name from Livorno (also known as Leghorn).

Size: 4 lbs. (female), 5 lbs. (male)

Number of eggs per week: Excellent

Egg Color: White

Egg Size: Large

Classification: Mediterranean

Comb Style: White birds have single combs. Some other colors have rose combs.

Temperament: Slightly nervous and can be flighty. Not the best choice if you are looking for a bird you can interact with easily. Leghorns are used as a cross in many modern breeds and when bred with a calmer bird, the temperament of their offspring improves.

Broody: No

Colors: Most commonly brown or white. Buff, black, silver, and other colors are available, though rare.

MARAN: Developed in France, this breed is prized for its beautiful dark brown, coppery eggs.

Size: 7 lbs. (female), 8 lbs. (male)

Number of eggs per week: Good

Egg Color: Dark Brown

Egg Size: Large

Classification: Continental

Comb Style: Single

Temperament: Calm and quiet.

Broody: Yes

Colors: Black, Cuckoo.

NAKED NECK: As its name implies, this odd looking chicken doesn't have feathers on its neck. In fact, it has almost half the feathers of other breeds its size. Also known as a Turken.

Size: 6 lbs. (female), 8 lbs. (male)

Number of eggs per week: Good

Egg Color: Tinted to Light Brown

Egg Size: Medium

Classification: All Other

Comb Style: Single

Temperament: Calm, active, yet easy to handle.

Broody: Yes

Colors: Black, white and red are recognized by the American Poultry Association. Other varieties are blue, cuckoo, or barred.

NEW HAMPSHIRE: This breed was developed from the Rhode Island Red. Also known as New Hampshire Red.

Size: 6 lbs. (female), 8 lbs. (male)

Number of eggs per week: Good

Egg Color: Brown

Egg Size: Extra Large

Classification: American

Comb Style: Single

Temperament: Docile, friendly and does not mind being handled.

Broody: Yes

Color: Light Reddish Brown

ORPINGTON: One of the smartest breeds. Believe it or not, some owners claim they are able to teach their Orpington tricks.

Size: 8 lbs. (female), 10 lbs. (male)

Number of eggs per week: Good

Egg Color: Light Brown

Egg Size: Large

Classification: English

Comb Style: Single

Temperament: Exceptionally docile

Broody: Sometimes

Colors: The original colors of black, white, buff, and blue are the most popular. Other colors are available and are still being developed.

PLYMOUTH ROCK: Known as "the chicken your grandma had", Plymouth Rocks originated in the United States and get their name from the town of Plymouth. After WWII, they became the most popular breed in America.

Size: 7 lbs. (female), 9 lbs. (male)

Number of eggs per week: Good

Classification: American

Egg Color: Brown

Egg Size: Large

Comb Style: Single

Temperament: Docile and friendly.

Broody: Yes. Make good mothers.

Colors: They come in several varieties, barred (black with white "barring"), buff and white being the most common. Other colors are partridge, silver laced, blue, and Columbian.

REDCAP: This bird sports a huge red comb, hence its name. Also known as the Derbyshire Redcap.

Size: 6 lbs. (female), 7 lbs. (male)

Number of eggs per week: Good

Egg Color: White

Egg Size: Medium

Classification: English

Comb Style: Rose

Temperament: Somewhat wild.

Broody: No

Color: Reddish brown to bluish-black.

RED STAR: This breed is a sex-link, meaning that it can be sexed based on its color immediately after hatching. Female chicks are buff or brown/red and male chicks are white. Red Stars are created by crossing a red hen with a White Rock, Silver Laced Wyandotte, Delaware, or Rhode Island White. Unlike many breeds, they will produce heavily through hot and cold weather. They sometimes go by the names Production Red, Golden Buff, Comet, Golden Comet, Golden Sex Link, and Isa Brown. Sex link chickens are not recommended as breeding stock since there is no way to know which characteristics they will pass along to their offspring.

Size: 5 lbs. (female), 6 lbs. (male)

Number of eggs per week: Excellent

Egg Color: Brown

Egg Size: Large to Extra Large

Classification: Not recognized

Comb Style: Single

Temperament: Easy going.

Broody: No

Color: Reddish brown with small areas of white sprinkled throughout.

RHODE ISLAND RED or WHITE: The official state bird of Rhode Island. It dates back to the mid 1840's, making it one of the oldest breeds in America.

Size: 6 lbs. (female), 8 lbs. (male)

Number of eggs per week: Excellent

Egg Color: Brown

Egg Size: Large

Classification: American

Comb Style: Single

Temperament: Good natured and docile.

Broody: No

Colors: Reddish-brown. There is also a White Rhode Island, though not as common.

SUSSEX: This breed was developed in the county of Sussex. Prior to the development of the Cornish Cross, the Sussex was the meat bird of choice in England.

Size: 7 lbs. (female), 9 lbs. (male)

Number of eggs per week: Good

Egg Color: Tinted to Light Brown

Egg Size: Medium

Classification: English

Comb Style: Single

Temperament: Calm, docile and curious.

Broody: Yes

Colors: Speckled, Red, Light

WELSUMMER (or WELSUMER): This breed takes its name from the village of Welsum, Holland. They lay dark brown eggs, often with speckles. Incidentally, the rooster on the Corn Flakes box was a Welsummer.

Size: 6 lbs. (female), 7 lbs. (male)

Number of eggs per week: Good

Egg Color: Brown

Egg Size: Large

Classification: Continental

Comb Style: Single

WYANDOTTE: An American breed that is a favorite among backyard chickens keepers because of the large number of color possibilities.

Size: 6 lbs. (female), 8 lbs. (male)

Number of eggs per week: Good

Egg Color: Brown or tinted

Egg Size: Large

Classification: American

Comb Style: Rose

Temperament: Friendly and make good pets.

Broody: Sometimes

Colors: They come in seventeen colors. The most common being silver laced, golden laced, white, black, buff, partridge, silver penciled, Columbian, and blue.

CLIMATE CONSIDERATIONS – HEAT TOLERANT BREEDS

A handful of breeds are heat tolerant but not especially cold tolerant. Most bantams, because of their small size, do well in heat. In general, standard size breeds with lighter feathering and smaller bodies, fare better in high temperatures. If you live in a particularly warm part of the world, the following breeds would be perfect for your climate, but would not fare well in cold climates.

ANDALUSIAN: Sometimes called the Blue Andalusian, this breed originated in the Andalucia region of Spain. Oddly, when two blues are bred, the result is some whites and some blacks, making this breed rare except among poultry enthusiasts.

Number of eggs per week: Good

Egg Color: White

Egg Size: Large

Classification: Mediterranean

Comb Style: Single

Temperament: Flighty

Broody: No

Colors: The color recognized by the American Poultry Association is blue. They also can be black and mottled.

CATALANA: The Catalana was developed in the district of Catalonia Spain, which is near Barcelona. The breed is more popular in South American and Spain than in the United States.

Size: 6 lbs. (female), 8 lbs. (male)

Number of eggs per week: Good

Egg Color: White to tinted

Egg Size: Medium

Classification: Mediterranean

Comb Style: Single

Temperament: Active and avoids people.

Broody: No

Color: Buff

CREVECOEUR: This beautiful bird with a showy black crest gets its name from Crève-Coeur en Ange, a small town in Normandy, France. It is thought to be one of the oldest French breeds.

Size: 6 lbs. (female), 8 lbs. (male)

Number of eggs per week: Good

Egg Color: White

Egg Size: Medium

Classification: Continental

Comb Style: V-shaped

Temperament: Quiet and easy to handle.

Broody: No

Color: Black

MINORCA: This breed gets its name from the Island of Minorca off the coast of Spain. It is sometimes called the "Red Faced Black Chicken" because of its red face and large red wattle and comb.

Size: 7 lbs. (female), 9 lbs. (male)

Number of eggs per week: Excellent

Egg Color: White

Egg Size: Extra Large

Classification: Mediterranean

Comb Style: Single and Rose

Temperament: Avoids human contact.

Broody: No

Colors: Black, White, Buff

PENEDESENCA: Unlike most chickens with white earlobes, this Spanish breed does not lay white eggs. In fact, they are known for their beautiful dark brown eggs.

Size: 4 lbs. (female), 5 lbs. (male)

Number of eggs per week: Good

Egg Color: Dark Brown

Egg Size: Medium

Classification: Not recognized

Comb Style: Carnation

Temperament: Flighty and excitable.

Broody: Yes

Colors: Creole, Wheaten, Partridge, Black

POLISH: This breed is known for its comical bouffant crest feathers that give it a Phyllis Diller look. Comes in bearded and beardless varieties.

Size: 4 lbs. (female), 6 lbs. (male)

Number of eggs per week: Good

Egg Color: White

Egg Size: Medium

Classification: Continental

Comb Style: V-Shaped

Temperament: Somewhat flighty and often on the bottom of the pecking order.

Broody: No

Colors: Black, White, Golden, Silver, Buff Laced

SICILIAN BUTTERCUP: This bird comes from Sicily and wears a cup shaped comb.

Size: 5 lbs. (female), 6 lbs. (male)

Number of eggs per week: Good

Egg Color: White

Egg Size: Medium

Classification: Mediterranean

Comb Style: Buttercup

Temperament: Flighty

Broody: No

Color: Buff with black spots.

CLIMATE CONSIDERATIONS –
HEAT AND COLD TOLERANT BREEDS

The following breeds are hardy in both hot and cold climates.

AMERAUCANA: Sometimes confused with Easter Eggers or
Americanas, which are mixed breeds that also lay colored eggs.
Ameraucanas are a purebred breed. Be sure to check the spelling before
you accidentally purchase an Americana thinking that it is an Ameraucana.
Size: 5 lbs. (female), 6 lbs. (male)
Number of eggs per week: Good
Egg Color: Green or Blue
Egg Size: Large
Classification: All Other
Comb Style: Pea
Temperament: Calm and not afraid of people.
Broody: Yes
Colors: Black, Blue, Blue-wheaten, Brown-red, Buff, Silver, Wheaten,
White

ANCONA: This breed gets its name from its original breeding place, Ancona, Italy. They arrived in the United States in the late 1800's and became a popular breed.

Size: 4 lbs. (female), 6 lbs. (male)

Number of eggs per week: Excellent

Egg Color: White

Egg Size: Large

Classification: Mediterranean

Comb Style: Rose and Single

Temperament: Have some wild tendencies and are a bit flighty.

Broody: No

Color: Black with white mottling.

AUSTRALORP: This breed originated in Australia, as the name suggests, and was developed from England's Black Orpington. In the 1920's, the breed set a world record for most eggs laid in a year (364). Size: 6 lbs. (female), 8 lbs. (male)

Number of eggs per week: Excellent

Egg Color: Brown

Egg Size: Large

Classification: English

Comb Style: Single

Temperament: Sweet, good natured chickens that make excellent pets and are good around children. They do not mind being handled and enjoy being petted.

Broody: Can be broody. Good mother.

Color: Shiny black feathers with iridescent green and purple highlights that glisten in sunlight.

BRAHMA: One of the larger breeds, this chicken is known as The Gentle Giant because of its exceptionally calm, friendly demeanor.

Size: 9 lbs. (female), 12 lbs. (male)

Number of eggs per week: Good

Egg Color: Brown

Egg Size: Large

Classification: Asiatic

Comb Style: Pea

Temperament: Extremely gentle and tame.

Broody: Yes

Colors: Light, Dark, Buff

CALIFORNIA GRAY: Cross between a White Leghorn and a Barred Plymouth Rock that was developed in California in the 1930's.

Size: 4 lbs. (female), 5 lbs. (male)

Number of eggs per week: Good

Egg Color: White

Egg Size: Large

Classification: Not recognized

Comb Style: Single

Temperament: Docile and can be held.

Broody: No

Color: Barred Gray/White

CALIFORNIA WHITE: Cross between a White Leghorn hen and a California Gray rooster.

Size: 5 lbs. (female), 7 lbs. (male)

Number of eggs per week: Excellent

Egg Color: White

Egg Size: Large

Classification: Not recognized

Comb Style: Single

Temperament: Quiet and easy to handle.

Broody: No

Color: White

DELAWARE: This breed originates from Delaware. It was once quite common, but is now endangered.

Size: 6 lbs. (female), 8 lbs. (male)

Number of eggs per week: Good

Egg Color: Brown

Egg Size: Large

Classification: American

Comb Style: Single

Temperament: Friendly and calm.

Broody: Yes

Color: White body with light black barring on the hackle, wings and tail.

LA FLECHE: This French breed is also known as the "Devil Bird" because its V-shaped comb resembles horns.

Size: 6 lbs. (female), 8 lbs. (male)

Number of eggs per week: Good

Egg Color: White

Egg Size: Large

Classification: Continental

Comb Style: V-Shaped

Temperament: Does not like human contact and acts slightly wild.

Broody: No

Colors: Its official color is black, though it also comes in blue, white, and cuckoo.

LEGHORN: Because they are prolific layers, most commercially produced eggs come from Leghorns. They originated in Italy and get their name from Livorno (also known as Leghorn).

Size: 4 lbs. (female), 5 lbs. (male)

Number of eggs per week: Excellent

Egg Color: White

Egg Size: Large

Classification: Mediterranean

Comb Style: White birds have single combs. Some other colors have rose combs.

Temperament: Slightly nervous and can be flighty. Not the best choice if you are looking for a bird you can interact with easily. Leghorns are used as a cross in many modern breeds and when bred with a calmer bird, the temperament of their offspring improves.

Broody: No

Colors: Most commonly brown or white. Buff, black, silver, and other colors are available, though rare.

MARAN: Developed in France, this breed is prized for its beautiful dark brown, coppery eggs.

Size: 7 lbs. (female), 8 lbs. (male)

Number of eggs per week: Good

Egg Color: Dark Brown

Egg Size: Large

Classification: Continental

Comb Style: Single

Temperament: Calm and quiet.

Broody: Yes

Colors: Black, Cuckoo.

NAKED NECK: As its name implies, this odd looking chicken doesn't have feathers on its neck. In fact, it has almost half the feathers of other breeds its size. Also known as a Turken.

Size: 6 lbs. (female), 8 lbs. (male)

Number of eggs per week: Good

Egg Color: Tinted to Light Brown

Egg Size: Medium

Classification: All Other

Comb Style: Single

Temperament: Calm, active, yet easy to handle.

Broody: Yes

Colors: Black, white and red are recognized by the American Poultry Association. Other varieties are blue, cuckoo, or barred.

REDCAP: This bird sports a huge red comb, hence its name. Also known as the Derbyshire Redcap.

Size: 6 lbs. (female), 7 lbs. (male)

Number of eggs per week: Good

Egg Color: White

Egg Size: Medium

Classification: English

Comb Style: Rose

Temperament: Somewhat wild.

Broody: No

Color: Reddish brown to bluish-black.

WHERE ARE THE CHICKENS

Now that you have a good idea of what chicken breed(s) you are interested in raising, you need to find a place to buy them. There are a number of options when shopping for chickens.

Start with fertile eggs and hatch them in an incubator.
Fertile eggs are available locally and online from breeders and hatcheries.

Purchase day old chicks.
There are many online hatcheries that sell day old chicks and ship them through the mail. Fortunately, chicks are able to live without food and water for 72 hours after hatching because they are still ingesting their yolk sacs. Many times, the minimum order from a hatchery is 25. The reason for this is that the chicks will stay warm in a large group while they make their journey through the mail system. Unless you plan on starting a full blown chicken farm, that's a lot of chickens! Some farm supply stores take orders for chickens in the spring. This is a good way to go if you don't need 25 chickens, as they will easily be able to place an order that meets the minimum. Farm supply stores also sell chicks in the spring, though the selection is not as good as it is from an online hatchery. Typically, farm

supply stores will have 3-5 fairly standard breeds available at a time. This is a great way to pick out the most active, and healthiest, chicks firsthand.

Purchase started pullets.

Started, or point of lay, pullets are birds that are 16-18 weeks old and are about to start laying. Most breeds start laying at 20-22 weeks. This is a great option for those of you who are impatient or don't want the hassle of hatching eggs or caring for young chicks. There are a few hatcheries that sell point of lay birds, but these are probably better purchased locally from a reputable breeder or farm, as they are quite expensive when ordered from an online hatchery.

HAPPY CHICKEN KEEPING

I hope you found the information in this book helpful and I wish you the best with your chicken keeping venture. I know your new chickens will bring you as much joy and satisfaction as mine have brought me. I urge you to continue your chicken research and to view some of these beautiful birds in person, in books, or on the internet.

If you have any questions or comments about this book or about raising chickens, don't hesitate to contact me at www.modernstead.com... a guide for small-scale homesteaders who want to live a simple, more self-sufficient life that nourishes both the body and the soul.